GOD'S MISSION: HEALING THE NATIONS

GOD'S MISSION: HEALING THE NATIONS

by

Dr David Burnett

MARC Europe
Evangelical Missionary Alliance
Send The Light Books

Burnett, David
    God's Mission: Healing the Nations
    1. Evangelistic work
    I. Title
    269'.2   BV3790

    ISBN 0-947697-46-2 (MARC)
         0-9502968-6-4 (EMA)
         0-903843-94-3 (STL)

Unless so marked, Scripture quotations in this publication are from the Holy Bible, New International Version. Copyright © 1973, 1978, 1984, International Bible Society. Published in Britain by Hodder and Stoughton. Used by permission.

MARC Europe is an integral part of World Vision, an international humanitarian organisation. MARC's object is to assist Christian leaders with factual information, surveys, management skills, strategic planning and other tools for evangelism. MARC also publishes and distributes related books on mission, church growth, management, spiritual maturity and other topics.

STL Books are published by Send The Light (Operation Mobilisation), PO Box 48, Bromley, Kent, England.

The Evangelical Missionary Alliance is a fellowship of evangelical missionary societies, agencies and training colleges that are committed to world mission. Its aims are to encourage cooperation and provide coordination between member societies and colleges, and to assist local churches to fulfil their role in world mission. The EMA offices are at Whitefield House, 186 Kennington Park Road, London SE11 4BT.

Typeset in Britain for MARC Europe, Cosmos House, 6 Homesdale Road, Bromley, Kent BR2 9EX by Furlonger Phototext, Victoria Chambers, Fir Vale Road, Bournemouth, Dorset BH1 2JN and printed by Richard Clay, Bungay, Suffolk MR35 1ED.

PROLOGUE

The angel also showed me the river of the water of life, sparkling like crystal, and coming from the throne of God and of the Lamb and flowing down the middle of the city's street. On each side of the river was the tree of life, which bears fruit twelve times a year, once each month; and its leaves are for the healing of the nations.

Book of Revelation 22:1-2

TABLE OF CONTENTS

INTRODUCTION

I remember sitting in a student meeting listening to a missionary speaking about India. He was the first missionary I had ever met, and as a young Christian who had not been brought up to attend any church, I listened with considerable perplexity. I suppose that I had always considered that missionaries had died out with the Victorian era. With them had gone the topee which was so characteristic of the British Empire, together with the line of native porters who had accompanied missionaries through uncharted jungles and inhospitable deserts.

Such pictures seemed strangely incongruous and irrelevant to the news reports which flash around the world in the later part of the twentieth century. What has a missionary to say to this modern world? Is he or she no more than a hold-over from a former age that should have by rights become extinct?

As I was pondering, the speaker continued with his talk and his slides. It was amid this activity that I felt another quiet, persistent voice speak to me. Not an audible voice, it was nevertheless a communication which broke into my thinking. The best way that I can express this communication in words is in the form of a request, 'David, what I have done in your life, I want to do in the lives of other people, and I want you to be my co-worker.' I had only been a Christian a few weeks, and I was deeply conscious of what God had done in my life. From being a University rebel I had changed, and God had given me fulfilment and meaning to life. I could understand that God would want others to enter into that fullness of life. But what shattered me was the thought that God wanted me to be a co-worker with Him.

'Why me?' I was only just starting to read the Bible for

the first time. Why did God not choose some of the other students who were at the same meeting? They had been brought up to go to Sunday school and to read the Bible, but I had done neither. The first question was quickly followed by a second. 'What does he want me to do?' I had never realised that by becoming a Christian God wanted me to do anything, and especially anything for him. Surely, he was the one who had done everything for me!

There was no appeal at the meeting; I did not even speak to the missionary, but for me it was the beginning of a journey. It was to be not only a journey of understanding the Bible, but also a journey that within five years would take me as a missionary to India. It was a journey that would present many questions, perhaps the greatest of which was to be, 'What is the missionary task to which the Church, and I as part of that Church, have been called?'

This book is a product of that journey of exploration. It is an attempt by one who has known the call of God to be a missionary to endeavour to understand that call, and to see its relevance in this age. It is my hope that as the readers consider the issues discussed in the text and reflect on the questions, they will come to a better understanding of the nature of mission and their role within that task.

David G Burnett
1986

1

FOUNDATIONS

It was my first week's teaching at a bible college in Madras. My wife and I were the only non-Indians on the staff, and we were eager to help the students grow in their Christian life. I was asked to teach Systematic Theology and was duly given a syllabus very similar to that which I had studied at home in England. I entered into teaching the course with great enthusiasm, starting with the doctrine of God as I was required.

We considered the so-called rational proofs for the existence of God: the ontological, cosmological, and teleological arguments. The students made detailed notes of what I said, but I slowly began to realise that no one in my class ever doubted the possible non-existence of God, and neither did almost the total population of India. The proofs for the existence of God were answers to questions that were being asked by Europeans, but not by Indians.

The sort of questions that my students were concerned about were issues such as healing, bhuts (ghosts), festivals, and poverty. The theology that I was trying to teach did not deal with these issues. The real questions of these students were very different from the usual questions that a white middle-class English student was asking of the Bible. However, I found that the Bible was not silent in giving answers to their questions as well as to mine.

The tremendous changes that have occurred during this century have raised new and challenging questions for Christians. None has been so great as that of the relationship which the Church has with society and the world. The questions being asked today by both Christians and non-Christians take many forms: 'What is the Church to do?' 'Why is the Church here in the world?' — or more basically for every individual Christian — 'What is God wanting of me?'

One cannot begin to answer these questions without reference to the word 'mission'. Throughout its history the Church has been conscious that it has been commissioned by God for a particular task — a task that is intimately involved with the purposes of God for his creation. However, as soon as one considers such a commonly used word as 'mission', one is quickly confronted with a divergence of understanding, not only of the concept of mission, but also of its very goal.

As John Stott[1] has clearly described, there are two extreme views concerning the nature of mission. The traditional view has been to equate mission with evangelism, and with the work of overseas missionaries. Here mission is seen as the verbal proclamation of the Good News to those who have never heard. Its emphasis lies on 'saving men's souls' to the neglect of their bodies. On the other hand, there is a second extreme which has an understanding of mission in a much wider and more general sense. God is seen at work in the whole of history, his aim being to bring a sense of peace and harmony that will embrace all peoples. In this case mission is seen primarily in terms of the social responsibility of the Church to the world. Between these two extremes lies a wide range of opinions and views.

The Latin root from which the English word 'mission' is derived means 'to send'. In this phrase lies the core to the discussion. Mission describes what the Church is sent into the world to do. This is not just a matter of academic interest to the theologian, but of great practical importance to all Christians. Emil Brunner has written that the Church exists by mission as a fire does by burning. Mission is not merely the application of theology taught in a classroom. Mission lies at the core of theology, and within the very character and action of God himself.

New Questions — Old Answers

The divergence of thinking on the nature of mission has

12

resulted from a series of major events during the last few centuries. We need to comprehend the major movements within world history that have moulded this thinking among Christians, and also to examine the current state of the Church in the world.

The dynamic growth of the early Church within the Roman Empire is well known, as is the eventual conversion of that great empire to Christianity. Less well appreciated are the effects on the Christian Church of the explosive growth of Islam in the seventh century. The Church in North Africa was mostly swept away by Islam, and the Persian Empire to the east was converted to that faith. The geographical result was that Europe, the heartland of Christianity, was locked into the area west of the Ural mountains. To the south and the east, Christianity was surrounded by Islam, to the north by the Arctic, and to the west the Atlantic Ocean.

Perhaps more significant than its geographical constraints was that Christianity became locked into the European cultural context. The great theological debates over the next thousand years were to occur within European cultures almost oblivious to the majority of the world — which knew little of Christianity. The theologies formulated were from the viewpoint of European societies which were at least nominally Christian.

The discovery of the sea routes in the seventeenth century meant that Christian nations were then able to circumnavigate the Muslim world. They discovered the New World of the Americas, and so began the massive migration of the Europeans to these countries. Contact was made with rich and ancient civilisations such as those of India and China. Strange exotic peoples were discovered who practised what appeared to be even stranger religions. The theological questions of how one related to such people had not previously been considered, because the questions had simply not been asked. Christian theology was basically European theology, which had developed from questions that European people had asked as a result of their own background.

Missionaries were already working among these non-

European peoples, and in some areas of the world many of the people were turning to Christianity. Questions concerning the nature of these new emerging churches faced the missionaries. They had to seek answers never sought by the former European theologians. How does one deal with aspects of cultures so different from one's own such as fetishism, ancestor worship, initiation rites and polygamy.

New trading links were forged between the Europeans and the rest of the world. The links brought wealth to European peoples to an extent never before known in history. How such wealth should be used became a crucial question to the peoples of so-called Christian Europe.

Exploration and trading raised two major issues which for many years the Church has failed to appreciate: culture and economics. As Christianity has spread out of the confines of European cultures, it has had to relate to various new cultures, and many of the traditional answers have been shown inadequate. Similarly, with the growth of the European economies the gap between the wealthy and the impoverished has faced the Church in a startling way. These two factors, culture and economics, will recur throughout this book because they influence in many ways the consideration of the missionary nature of the Church.

The Culture Factor

Culture has most simply been defined as the total way of life of a particular people. It includes the outward practical aspects of how a people obtain their food, how they dress, how they organise their society and marriage, as well as how they practise their religion, or what music they play. Culture also includes the language and religious beliefs of the society, both of which have great influence in forming the ideas of the people. At the core of any culture are those fundamental ideas assumed by the people to be true and, in general, above contradiction − ideas concerning space and time, gods and creation, what is good and what is evil. These fundamental ideas are usually called the 'worldview' of a society and enable the people to make sense and order of their environment.

Every child born into any society is essentially born cultureless, but during the first few years of life quickly gains an adequate understanding of the way of life of that people. This is sufficient to allow the child to acquire the combined experience and skill of former generations, enabling him to cope in his own culture with sufficient success. The many thousands of societies in the world each have their own cultures, and although many will have some aspects in common, no two cultures will be identical.

The whole topic of biblical interpretation is thus affected in two important ways. First, when God chose to reveal himself to mankind he did so in the culture, and therefore language, of the people to whom that revelation was given. If this had not been the case the communication would have been irrelevant and meaningless to them. However, God communicated through their own culture — even their own personality — so that his truth expresses itself through the writer's own character and culture. This was accomplished without corruption of God's revelation of truth.

Clearly, then, as one approaches the Scripture it is necessary to understand the cultural — and therefore the historical and religious conditions — of the Israelites who were at the focus of God's revelation to humankind; to study what the words and phrases would have meant to the people of that

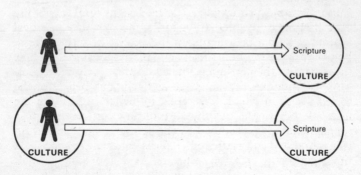

Fig 1:1
The Reading of Scripture in Relation to Culture

particular period. A good Bible translation will help, but it is still an advantage to study the way of life of the people of the Middle East during the period of biblical history.

A failure to appreciate this truth can lead to major confusion. In one rather isolated village in Africa a missionary was telling the story of the four men who brought their sick friend to Jesus. He told how these men could not approach Jesus directly because of the crowd and so climbed on to the roof; they lowered their friend through the roof to the very feet of Jesus, who healed the sick man. The villagers gasped with wonder. They were astonished not so much because of the healing of the man, but of the greater miracle of four men being able to stand on a roof. In their area of Africa all the roofs were steeply conical, and they knew nothing else. They were interpreting the story in terms of their own culture and experience. Although we may smile at the apparent naivety of the villagers, can we be sure that in our own reading of the Scriptures we are not coming to similar wrong conclusions because of our lack of understanding of the cultures of the Old and New Testaments?

This brings us to the second major consideration in biblical interpretation. Not only does the Scripture need to be read in its own cultural context, but the reader needs to appreciate that he is a product of his own culture. (See figure 1:1) When a person approaches the Scriptures he is looking for answers to issues of his society. There is a vast cultural difference between the patriarchs of the Old Testament and the modern Western city dwellers. As a result, much of what happened in the daily life of the patriarchs appears strange and totally irrelevant. A Turkana nomad from northern Kenya, however, would find many points of parallel with his own life. He too is concerned with his sheep and his camels as he looks for pasture for his flock.

The Bible provides a vast storehouse of answers to the needs of humanity, but one society will be asking different questions of the text than another. When Christians in a particular society develop their own theology – 'science of god' – it will therefore not be identical to that of another society. (See figure 1:2) One may well ask whether or not

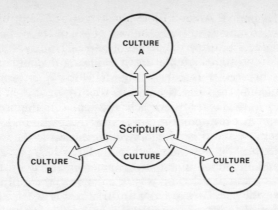

Fig 1:2

Understanding of Scripture in Relation to Culture

this makes truth itself relative? Should not Christians of whatever society have the same theology?

If two men standing on two sides of a mountain are looking to the peak, do they see the same mountain? There will be a difference in the rock forms and shape of the mountain. There may even be differences in the snow line and colour, but they are still looking at the same mountain. In the same way, Christians from different cultures may exhibit various differences, but one would expect certain fundamentals of the Christian truth to be common to all.

One society may see Christ as the one who brings meaning and relevance to human existence. Another society may appreciate Christ as the one who has delivered them from the power of Satan and the fear of witchcraft. Yet others may see him as the Truth among a bewildering array of religious options. Just as one man cannot see all the various views of the mountain at the same time, so no culture can claim to have the sum total of biblical perspective. One society may be 'blind' to some issues of biblical teaching that are highly relevant to other people. African friends have taught me much about the biblical teaching on spirits due to its particular relevance to their own culture.

The Economic Factor

The second issue which raises many questions today is that of wealth and poverty. When according to United Nations figures 800 million people are starving, and double that number are undernourished, some striking questions are being asked of the Church and its mission.

There have always been rich and poor in the world. However, the European expansion of the eighteenth and nineteenth centuries brought a new dimension to the world scene. When William Carey left for India in 1797, on average the standard of living in Britain (measured by food production and population) was on a par with that of India. By 1900, the standard of living in Britain was at least four times that of India, while today it is more like forty times. How has this come about?

The answer to this question depends much on one's analysis of the political scene. What is clear is that the trading links established during the seventeenth and eighteenth centuries brought cheap raw materials to the European nations, thus providing resources for the Industrial Revolution. Cheap machine-made products were then exported back to the non-Western world, making additional profits for European nations. The growing wealth of the European nations was linked to the future poverty of the non-Western world[2].

Ronald Sider's book, *Rich Christians in an Age of Hunger,*[3] has done much to alert the Western Church to its responsibilities to the hungry. Sider has challenged western lifestyle, the standard of living to which we have become accustomed in our culture. He has also challenged us with the needs of the poor. These issues link closely to the whole of the mission of the Church, especially as the countries traditionally known for sending missionaries are now the wealthy nations, while the receiving countries are poor.

Issues of culture and economics together confront the Church in its concern for mission and the means of mission. This book attempts to address some of the related questions, and to help readers formulate their own ideas as to the biblical view of God's mission in the world.

18

Approaching Mission

At the beginning of this century, a movement of scholarship termed 'biblical theology' developed. It took its impetus from the work of Karl Barth and has had a considerable influence in the study of theology. This approach seeks to study biblical themes in their historical and cultural context, as they develop in Scripture; it contrasts with systematic theology, which tends to identify various themes within Scripture as a whole.

Biblical theology is of particular significance for a study of mission because it deals with God's self-revelation in the course of history and in terms of particular cultural realities.[4] It is like following a stream from its spring in the mountains down into the valley where it grows as other streams join, until it becomes a river in full flood. (See figure 1:3) Likewise, with the developing awareness of the mission of the people of God, there is growing responsibility and privilege given by God to his people.

One major qualification will be made in the use of the method of biblical theology. Many of the exponents of this method have tended to contrast various portions of the Scriptures. For example, the writings of Paul have been contrasted with those of John. However, in this study, the Scriptures will be considered as a unity. In reading the Bible one cannot but be impressed by the remarkable unity and wholeness of the text, although it was written by many writers over a long period of time.

In 1522, Luther wrote, '. . . poor and of little value are the swaddling clothes [Old Testament], but dear is the Christ, the treasure that lies in them.'[5] But to believe in the full inspiration of the Scriptures means that the Old Testament is not just preparation but is a major portion of the revelation of God. The New Testament fulfils the Old, but does not replace it (I Cor 10:11).

Some societies will find that certain portions will be more relevant to them and their questions than other portions. Harold Turner in a study of the preaching of the African Independent Churches[6] found far greater reference to portions of Scripture dealing with healing and spirits than

19

GOD

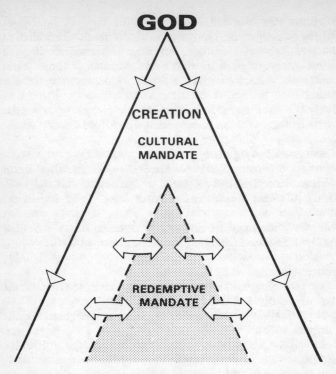

CREATION

**CULTURAL
MANDATE**

**REDEMPTIVE
MANDATE**

Fig 1:3

God's Self-Revelation in History and Culture

would ever be found in a western church. One must avoid, therefore, concentrating on a few popular texts, instead seeking an integrated approach to the subject of mission. For this reason, this study will not commence with the well known missionary passages, but will follow the stream from its mountain spring to the sea.

Discussion Questions
1   Why is the knowledge of the local culture necessary for Christian mission?

20

2   Read Revelation 3:14-22. List the various figures of speech or images used in the passage. What do they mean to you, and to your culture, on first impressions? Read a commentary, and see how an understanding of the cultural context of Laodicea gives a fuller understanding of the passage.

3   In the light of the definition of 'worldview', what are the main distinctive elements of your own culture?

Recommended Reading

John R W Stott, *Christian Mission in the Modern World* (Falcon Press: London, 1975).

James W Sire, *The Universe Next Door* (IVP: Leicester, 1977).

John R W Stott and Robert Coote, *Down to Earth — Studies in Christianity and Culture* (Hodder: London, 1980).

Footnotes

1   John Stott, *Christian Mission in the Modern World* (Falcon Books: London, 1975), pp 15-20.

2   P L Berger, *Pyramids of Sacrifice* (Pelican Books: London, 1977).

3   R J Sider, *Rich Christians in an Age of Hunger* (Hodder and Stoughton: London, 1977).

4   Geerhardus Vos, *Biblical Theology* (Banner of Truth Trust: Edinburgh 1975) pp 3-18.

5   Martin Luther, *Commentary on Genesis* (1522) (Concordia: St Louis, 1958).

6   Howard W Turner, *Profile through Preaching* (Edinburgh House Press: Edinburgh, 1965).

2

GOD, MAN, AND THE UNIVERSE

It was a hot, sunny day in south India as I was making my way quickly through the milling crowds of a busy village market to get to a meeting. I was familiar enough with the villages of India to neglect most of the noise, dust and flies that are so common. I saw a little space in the crowds and quickly stepped into it only to find that at my feet was a man. I almost fell over him because he was lying on the ground. He had no legs at all, only a cloth wrapped over the bottom part of his body. In a withered hand he held a begging bowl as he propelled himself along the ground with the other hand.

Lying on his back, this man was looking up at me. He lay among all the dirt, litter, and flies. Just for a moment we met, and then the crowds pushed us apart. Two men had met, be it only for a second, but I went away a different man. It was not the dirt or the deformity that I remember, but his eyes. In his eyes I saw that he was a man, with emotions and humanity like me — like me!

How did the world come into being? How was man created? Is there a Creator? These are some of the most fundamental questions that any may ask. Every society on earth has its own distinct answers to these questions — answers so often wrapped in poetic symbolism and stories which have been passed on from one generation to another.

Stories of the Creation must never be regarded simply as fables. The very stories themselves present various assumptions about God, humankind, and the universe. These are fundamental ideas about how people make order of the world about them and so influence what they consider to be morally good or bad, relevant or irrelevant.

The Zulus have the myth of *Umuveli Ngqange* (the one who first made his appearance), who came out of a reed. He brought out after him men and women, flowers and trees, birds and animals and all the fruit of the earth[1]. Likewise within the ancient world there were many stories of a creator, and of the way that he brought the world into being. Mesopotamian cosmology spoke of a creator-god who emerged from the primeval chaos, managed to conquer it and form it into a new order. Finally, out of the new order man finally appeared.

Although the biblical account of the Creation shows some similarities with the Mesopotamian story, it also has some important differences[2]. It does not major upon graphic symbolism but demonstrates a God who is totally different from his creation and rejects any notion of the plurality of gods. The first few chapters of Genesis sketch the outline of a worldview which is fundamental to our understanding of the religious ideas of the people of Israel.

As J Blauw has written, 'The first chapters of Genesis are (as is the whole book of Genesis, for that matter) a key to understanding all of the Old Testament and even, for those who recognise the unity of the Bible, of the whole Bible.'[3]

In order to understand the development of thought through the Bible one must first grasp the three major systems described in the Genesis account:

1 Man's relationship with God.
2 Man's relationship with man.
3 Man's relationship with the environment.

These systems provide the fundamental concepts within which the missionary task is to be undertaken.

God

The Bible presents a well defined, monotheistic view which is not particularly argued but simply assumed as logical and self-evident. In so doing it provides a highly developed ideology essential to all that is to be revealed. The existence of the supernatural is accepted as an essential aspect of such a worldview, and no allowance is made for the materialistic view that assumes the natural human senses can see and study *all* that exists.

The major assumptions in the Genesis account are as follows:

God is Creator God begins the disclosure of himself as the one who creates. Before the universe was created, God already existed, and whatever now exists does so because of God's will and creative power. There is no struggle with lesser gods, but a statement of authority and an emerging sequence of the Creation.

God is transcendent Because God created, he is utterly different from that which he has created. He did not create the universe as an extension of his own essence, but out of nothing. He is therefore totally unique. He is the absolute, and creation only finds its meaning in him.

God is personal Implicit here is the concept that God has power, knowledge and moral perfection. To have power is to be able to do things, and so be able to act in certain ways. The universe is not chaotic, but orderly. Cause and effect are real laws of nature, but they are not locked into a closed system. God is able to act within the flow of history to fulfil his purposes.

God is able to communicate Throughout the book of Genesis God is revealed as one who is concerned with his Creation. As Schaeffer has said, 'He is not silent'[4]. He has revealed himself in ways intelligible to man.

God is worthy of worship God, whatever else he may be, is seen as the supreme object of religious devotion. This is a key issue in the refinement of the theistic concept of God in the Old Testament.

These principles may seem familiar to the Westerner, but they are radical in the formation of the monotheistic view of the world. Any worldview with its particular set of presuppositions — held either consciously or unconsciously by a

24

people — provides a way of explaining the world. The first book of the Bible establishes its particular patterns and allows the development of vitally important principles which will affect the basis of biblical revelation. The religions of India (Hinduism and Buddhism), emphasising that man may discover God from within his own human spirit, tend to be mystical, allowing the development of a radically different worldview. These religions consequently tend to be world-denying, looking for release from a corrupt world, which is regarded as no more than illusion. Time is conceived of as no more than an endless cycle from which man looks for release.

In contrast, Christianity — along with Judaism — in recognising a God beyond Creation, emphasises the revelation of God to men from outside the human spirit. This prophetic notion is world-affirming and accepts the essential goodness of the material world and its future redemption. God is conceived of as one who is purposeful and at work in his creation. Time, therefore, is seen as a progress from the beginning to the completion of those purposes.

Man
The Genesis account is not primarily designed to tell us when and how man was created, but who created him and why.

The Image of God
A key issue in an understanding of the nature of man is found in the phrase made in the image and likeness of God (Gen 1:26). This phrase emphasises the distinctiveness of man from the rest of creation, and includes many issues essential to an understanding of Christian mission.

First, man is capable of knowing God and of having a relationship with him. There is a spiritual quality about all men which produces a hunger to know the deity and to communicate with him. All men therefore have the right to know their Creator; this truth, then, imposes an implicit obligation on mission.

Secondly, man is a personality. As Francis Schaeffer has so clearly expressed[5], here lies the answer that has plagued modern man: where do love and communication come from? The biblical answer focuses on God who was there as love and communication. Man created in his image manifests something of his nature and character.

Thirdly, man has an ability to create and reform his environment. Among the many options before him, man is able to choose and modify and create a way of life. As stated in the Wheaton '83 Statement, 'Culture is God's gift to human beings . . . As Creator, He made us creative. This creativity produces cultures.'[6]

Finally, man was created immortal, not only in the sense that he was endowed with endless life, but he was not subject to the law of death. As Paul writes, 'sin entered the world through one man' (Rom 5:12; I Cor 15:20,21). The Fall is to have a marked effect on the image of God in man's nature. See chapter 3.

The Unity of Man

Another important aspect of the Creation account is that humankind is from a common origin. 'From one man he made every nation of men, that they should inhabit the whole earth' (Acts 17:26). Racial variations are a fact of human existence, but these are subordinate to a common humanity. No individual or race may therefore consider itself above others.

It may here be necessary to distinguish the concepts of race and culture. These two concepts were once conceived of as inseparable, but now they are seen as distinct entities, though with possible overlap. Race depends on biological inheritance and results in particular characteristics such as skin and hair colour, height and skull shape. Culture, on the other hand, is a result of the social environment in which the individual grows up. It is learned, not just inherited biologically. Overlap results because people often tend to marry within their own societal group.

Many societies today still practise racism whether openly or overtly. But the received idea of racial superiority cannot be accepted in the light of the Genesis narrative. It is especially important for the cross-cultural missionary to understand this. The Uppsala conference of 1969[7] strongly condemned racism within the missionary enterprise.

Universe
The Creation was a demonstration of the very nature and character of God, as Paul points out in Romans 1:20, 'For since the creation of the world God's qualities – his eternal power and divine nature – have been clearly seen, being understood from what has been made, so that men are without excuse.' This verse lays down principles significant to the whole notion of mission.

Man Is an Integral Part of Nature
Christians in flight from the theories of evolution have stressed the distinctiveness of man; however, no matter how superior his intelligence and sophisticated his life, man is still part of creation. Genesis shows that man's origin is the climax of God's creative will. 'And the Lord God formed man from the dust of the ground and breathed into his nostrils the breath of life, and man became a living being' (Gen 2:7). Man's existence, therefore, is closely linked with nature. The world is not just an optional extra, but essential to man's continued existence.

Man Is Distinct from the Rest of Creation
In Genesis chapter 1 man is represented as the final stage of the expression of God's creative will. It is seen in what Calvin calls 'the language of deliberation'[8]. Instead of the simple 'Let there be . . .' (1:3; 6, 9, 11, 14, 15, 20, 24) there is the 'Let us make . . .' (1:26, 27). Man is unique from the rest of God's creation.

Nature Was Created Good
Six times in Genesis 1, one reads that God created nature and it was 'very good'. Nature is important in itself to God, and in some sense beyond its importance to man, God obtains pleasure from the world he has created. Several

passages in Scripture (Job 38; Ps 19: 1-4; Ps 96: 11-12; Ps 148) reveal God's pleasure in his creation. Harmony and balance characterised everything rightly related to the Creator. Clearly, God wants man to enjoy nature.

God's delight adds a new dimension to man's use of natural resources. Nature is not there simply to provide for man's material needs, but equally to provide him with pleasure — a principle fundamental to the Creation. On the other hand, nature is not to be seen as an object of worship for man. Man's vision must not just be limited to the wonders of nature, for such wonders are only meant to reflect the glory of the ultimate Creator.

As Hooykas has said, 'Nature is viewed not as a deity to be worshipped, but as a work of God to be admired, studied and managed.'[9]

The Cultural Mandate

The picture given in Genesis is one of harmony and balance within which man had certain responsibilities. The responsibilities placed on him before the Fall need to be distinguished from the redemptive purposes that God began to unfold after the Fall. Kuyper[10] called these two aspects the cultural mandate and the redemptive mandate.

While the cultural mandate can be seen as having three components[11] — marriage, work and government — the redemptive mandate is manifest in the work of Christ, and in his proclamation by the people of God. We must first consider the obligations placed upon the first man by his Creator.

Marriage

'Be fruitful and increase in number; fill the earth . . .' (Gen 1:28). God did not intend the first pair of human beings to remain in isolation, but to multiply and begin a society. To follow the directive to live all over the world would have clearly involved the migration of people. This has clearly happened, but with a projected world population of five billion by 2000 AD. One must ask, 'Is this what God intended?'

The word that is frequently translated 'fill', or as in the New International Version 'fill the earth', has a range of meanings. The first is like that of filling a cup, which is to fill to a defined limit. A river which is full in this sense is filled to its banks, but it has not overflowed. Secondly, the word translated 'fill' has in some contexts the notion of satisfaction. A hungry man will eat his fill and feel satisfied. Genesis 1:28 is not a licence for uncontrolled and unlimited expansion of the human population beyond the capacity of the area. The 'filling' should in fact be to the benefit and satisfaction of the land itself. Nature should be improved by its contact with man not made a wasteland!

Work

'The Lord God took the man and put him in the Garden of Eden to work it and take care of it' (Gen 2:15).

Few commands have been so misunderstood as this. As Max Nicholson has written: 'The first step must be plainly to reject and to scrub out the complacent image of man the conqueror of nature, and of man licensed by God to conduct himself as the Earth's worst pest. An intensive spell of environmental repentance is called for.'[12]

The word 'subdue' which is used in the RSV conveys the idea of a fight to conquer nature, but the actual meaning is to take the authority over the earth which is already possessed. In no sense can this command be interpreted as an exhortation to unfettered exploitation of the natural resources God has provided. God placed man in the world to look after it and preserve it from harm. 'The development of the Earth's resources is a Godlike activity; it is as though man were carrying on God's creative acts after him'.[13]

Government

As noted, this aspect of the cultural mandate is closely linked with the others. Man is given the freedom to act as God's vice-regent to rule over the world in a responsible way (see figure 2:1).

God gave to mankind power delegated for a particular end: the support of the human race and the development of

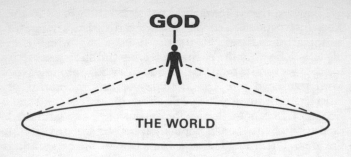

Fig 2:1
Man as God's Vice-Regent
in Creation and Culture

the resources of creation. These three aspects of the cultural mandate describe the 'mission' of the first men and women. However, it is essential to realise that even after the Fall this mission still remains, as seen in Genesis 9:1-7. This theme develops and enlarges as one continues through the Scriptures. It is the first of the streams of responsibility to join and grow to become a flowing river — which will define the missionary nature of the Church today.

Discussion Questions

1   The Earth is God's gift to humankind. What should be our attitude to the conservation of non-renewable sources of energy and minerals, of animal life in danger of extinction, and the precarious ecological balance of many natural habitats.

2   What exactly is wrong with apartheid? How best should Christians in South Africa — white or black — counter it?

3   The fact that God made work part of the cultural mandate shows that it is related to the essential dignity of humankind. What does this have to say about our personal attitude to work and unemployment?

Recommended Reading

Francis A Schaeffer, *Genesis in Space and Time* (Hodder: London, 1972).

Patrick Sookhdeo, Ed, *All One in Christ? — The Biblical View of Race* (Marshall, Morgan & Scott: London, 1974).

Albert M Wolters, *Creation Regained* (IVP: Leicester, 1986

Footnotes

1   Penny Miller, *Myths & Legends of South Africa* (Bulpin Publications: Cape Town, 1979) p 153.

2   R K Harrison, *Introduction to the Old Testament* (Tyndale Press: London, 1970) pp 454-7.

3   J Blauw, *The Missionary Nature of the Church* (Lutterworth Press: London, 1962) p 18.

4   Francis A Schaeffer, *He Is There and He Is Not Silent* (Tyndale House Publishers: Wheaton, 1972).

5   Francis A Schaeffer, *Escape From Reason* (IVP: Leicester, 1968).

6   Wheaton '83 Statement, Social Transformation: The Church in Response to Human Need. *Transformation* Vol 1, No 1 (1984): pp 23-28.

7   See entire volume of *International Review of Mission*, Vol 59, No 235 (1970).

8   John Calvin, *Commentaries on the Book of Genesis* Vol 1 (Calvin Translation Society: Edinburgh, 1847), p 91.

9   R Hooykas, *Religion and the Rise of Modern Science* (Eerdmans: Grand Rapids, 1972), p 9.

10   A Kuyper, *Encyclopedia of Sacred Theology* (MacMillan: New York, 1898). For a similar interpretation see Arthur Glasser, 'Confession Church Growth, and Authentic Unity in Missionary Strategy', *Protestant Crosscurrents in Mission*, N A Morner, ed (Abingdon Press: Nashville, 1968) pp 178-192.

11   Deitrich Bonhoeffer, *Ethics* (MacMillan: New York, 1965) pp 207-13.

12   Max Nicholson, Nature Conservancy leaflet.

13   Andrew Walls, 'Stewardship', *Handbook on World Development* (Shaftesbury Project Publication: Nottingham, 1983) pp 82-85

3

THE SPOILING OF
PARADISE

*Adam and Eve, dressed like peasants in bark-cloth, were seen
cultivating in the shade of a great tree. Adam became weary,
and throwing himself down, slept while Eve continued digging
with slow, tired movements. Then, far away one small drum
began to throb, menacing and horribly insistent; and to the
rhythm of it a girl, swathed in a scarlet cloth, with a long, green
train dragging behind her over the dry grass, danced out the
Temptation. It was an extraordinary dance of undulation and
slithering movement, with her two hands keeping up a ceaseless
flickering at the level of her eyes. And opposite her Eve also
danced her reluctant, frightened, slow surrender to fascination
and desire. Louder and louder grew the throbbing of the drum,
more intense the serpent's hatred until Eve, who was already
fondling the fruit that hung from the tree, suddenly tugged it
from the branch and sank her teeth into it. At that instant the
drum was silenced, and the snake slid quickly away into the
surrounding darkness.*[1]

Eden was described in Genesis as a garden — beautiful and
useful. It was within this context that God presented man
with one of two options: either to remain in a face-to-face
relationship with God as his vice-regent, or to choose an
unknown, separate existence from within the Creation.

The Fall
The historicity of the Fall has been subject to much critical
study during this century. After a comprehensive study of
various principles of interpretation, R K Harrison prefers to
regard such narratives as 'religious drama'. He writes, 'This

32

definition helps to preserve the form which is essential to the content, without at the same time casting any doubt, historical or otherwise, upon the basic truths enshrined in the narratives themselves.'[2] It is important not to confuse the issues of a historical fall with the narrative structure in which that truth was conveyed. In the Genesis account, Man was permitted by God to exercise his authority, but God placed upon him one restriction. Man was able to eat of all the fruit of the garden except that from one tree. In the scope of his natural existence this was a minor prohibition, but from within the context of his moral responsibility to God as Creator it is of supreme importance. As Calvin has expressed it '. . . man was governor of the world, with the exception, that he should, nevertheless, be subject to God. A law is imposed upon him in token of his subjection . . . Therefore, the prohibition of the tree was the test of obedience.'[3] Man was required by God to act responsibly with respect to nature, according to the inner moral construction of the universe.

The Nature of Man's Disobedience

God's command was not unexplained nor unreasonable but had been presented rationally and Adam and Eve had been warned about the outcome. The first moral test came in terms of man's relationship with nature. The fruit of a tree constituted the test of obedience, and as such it was something basic to man's bodily need. Secondly, the temptation came to man through a created being − a serpent. Man's mistake was to listen to something created rather than to the Creator himself. The seduction was achieved not by some supernatural manifestation, but through an animal in the garden.

The Serpent

'Now the serpent was more crafty than any of the wild animals that the Lord God had made' (Gen 3:1). Immediately this phrase raises a host of questions to which one finds no clear answers within the Bible. The Bible, however, is a book which gives revelation about salvation and is not an exhaustive text on the created order.

As the biblical narrative continues, complex information is revealed about the person of the tempter and his activities. It is here sufficient, however, to realise that within the created order there are even now forces opposed to God. These forces have personality and are part of the created order, and as such they will have an influence on the natural world. (See further discussion in chapters 8 and 22.)

Adam, listening to the serpent, rejected the role of vice-regent with the responsibility 'to guard' God's creation. He showed himself willing to be directed by the creation, and not by the Creator. He therefore refused to carry out the mission of the cultural mandate under God's direction and for God's glory. The fruit was eaten!

Results of the Fall

The outcome of this act of disobedience is clearly stated in Romans 5:12: 'Therefore, just as sin entered the world through one man, and death through sin, and in this way death came to all men, because all have sinned.' In this way a new dimension was introduced to the whole context of mission; God's creation was marred.

The reaction of God to this disobedience was judgement which fell on all parties. First, God cursed the serpent, and thus also all the supernatural forces which would oppose God. Yet even within the curse there is hope for mankind in the woman's 'offspring', who will deal a death-blow to the serpent. Evil did not originate within the world of humankind, but from the supernatural realm, an important issue as we consider evil in the world today.

Secondly, man's relationship with God was fractured. The significance of the act for Adam and Eve was that they began to feel fear and guilt and so tried to hide from God (Gen 3:10). The open communication that they had had with God became of itself a thing to avoid. Adam and Eve were put out of Eden, and God now began to direct the course of human history, not for man's contentment, but for his restoration. In this fact we have at least a partial answer to the question of why God allows suffering in the world — a question to which I will return in Chapter 10.

Thirdly, woman's relationship with man was affected in two ways (Gen 3:16). On the one hand, pain was greatly increased in childbearing. On the other hand, although a woman would continue to have sexual desires for her husband, she will be ruled over by him. What is therefore established is a new pattern of social relationships in a fallen world.

Fourthly, the effect of the Fall came upon all aspects of creation, including the earth itself. The earth now only yields its fruit with reluctance and unreliability. The history of agricultural development illustrates the issue. No sooner has one problem been solved than another occurs in its place. The balance of nature that existed before the Fall allowed man readily and effectively to provide for his needs with maximum return. Now weeds and pests become a major factor, and it is only by hard work that man is able to provide for his needs. As Paul writes 'For we know that the whole creation has been groaning, as in the pains of childbirth' (Rom 8:22).

Finally, with regard to man himself there is death and the dissolution of the individual. The Hebrew notion of personality is different from that of the Greeks. The Platonic view of man was that of a spirit entombed within a body, and so death offered release. For the Hebrews man was seen as a total being — a living soul. Death can then be viewed as consisting of three steps. First it was an immediate separation from the presence of God. Secondly comes physical death when an individual's component parts will be dissolved in the earth. Thirdly, there is eternal death as the ultimate penalty given by God.

For man created in the image of God it meant that the 'image' was smashed. It was like a mirror that has been dropped and has fractured into a multitude of pieces. However, it is necessary to note that the image was not totally lost. Man in a particular way still shows something of the divine image, and still has within him the potential to fulfil the cultural mandate.

35

The reformed theologians used the expression 'Total depravity'. This has been misunderstood by many but it never meant that man was thoroughly depraved, nor that humankind cannot admire beauty and goodness. It was meant to indicate that every part of man's nature was infected by the inherent corruption of sin.[4] Man still has the potential to produce that which is beautiful and good; but even at its highest, man's nature is marred. (See also Norman Anderson's comment on p47-48.)

The Flood

The Wickedness of Mankind

Both the blessings and the curses of Genesis 1-3 are extended in Genesis 4-11 throughout the Earth. One sees acts of goodness, but also acts of cruelty and evil. Abel offers a sacrifice to God; Cain kills his brother. Music and culture grew up, but at the same time Lamech boasted of his cruel vengeance (Gen 4:17-24).

The human family began to grow and spread out across the world. The family became a people as recorded in the genealogies of Genesis 5. However, at this point comes a refrain that is to echo down through human history, 'and died . . .' (Gen 5:5, 8, 11, 14, 17, 20, 27, 31); God's curse was now being fulfilled upon humankind. The growth of population seemed to lead to an explosion of evil in the world. 'The Lord saw how great man's wickedness on the Earth had become, and that every inclination of the thoughts of his heart was only evil all the time. The Lord was grieved that he had made man on the Earth, and his heart was filled with pain' (Gen 6:5, 6).

The Wrath of God

There is one story which is surprisingly common to the mythology of many peoples in the world and that is of a flood. Archaeological studies by Woolley, and others, have shown that Mesopotamia suffered a number of devastating floods at different periods in antiquity. From the available evidence it would seem reasonable to conclude that the record in Genesis constitutes one such flood of major proportions that occurred in a localised area. Several versions of the flood narrative were in existence in the third millennium BC. The significance of the biblical account is that it had a basis in morality. The Genesis story confronts us with the judgement of God and in so doing introduces some notable insights into the whole nature of the missionary task.

The concept of a God of wrath is unpopular today even among Christians. More popular is the notion of the love of God; whereas in fact both aspects are important in Scripture. This unpopularity is partly due to a misunderstanding of the very nature of the wrath of God. Two errors are frequently held by Christians. First, God's wrath is equivalent to that of man's anger with all its spitefulness, bad temper and irritability. But God is not a bad-tempered old man; he is holy. The second common error is to see God's wrath as merely the inevitable result of laws of cause and effect within God's moral universe. God's anger is not just the operation of some moral law in his creation. It is a personal quality of God without which God would cease to be fully righteous and his love would degenerate into mere sentimentality.

R G V Tasker[5] defines the wrath of God as 'the permanent attitude of the holy and just God when confronted by sin and evil.' This anger is not a spiteful reaction, but an unchanging expression to all that is contrary to his holy love. 'The wrath of God is being revealed from heaven against all the godlessness and wickedness of men who suppress the truth by their wickedness' (Rom 1:18). Time and time again the biblical narrative will reveal the cycle of man's sin followed by God's judgement, man's repentance and then his restoration in blessing. The wrath of God is an essential aspect of the whole of God's dealing with man.

The wrath of God shows first that God takes sin seriously in whatever form it manifests itself, and so must the Christian in considering the nature of the Church's mission. God will not persevere with those who persist in sin. As with the Amorites, judgement would come when their sin reached its full measure (Gen 15: 16). This judgement even extended to his own chosen people Israel, who were eventually taken into Exile. But God's judgement is tempered with mercy: 'But Noah found favour in the eyes of the Lord' (Gen 6:8). As the letter to the Hebrews reveals, Noah was not saved by his works, but by the faith that he exercised resulting in the fact that he obeyed God (Heb 11:7; 2 Peter 2:5).

Another important aspect of the story of the Flood is the fact that although only Noah was found righteous, his whole family was saved. Salvation may be on an individual basis, but God is concerned about families and whole societies; God made man as a social being and is aware of that dimension of man. The sin or righteousness of an individual will have its effect on the society of which he or she is a member.

The Covenant with Noah (Gen 9:1-7)
After God's judgement was executed God gave to this family a new opportunity and entered into a new relationship with them. This covenant is important because it is to relate to all of humanity from the time of Noah. Jewish theologians stress the point that the Gentiles are under this covenant even until today.

There are several characteristics to the covenant:

It is universal — God's pledge to Noah includes all mankind, and all living creation, 'all those that came out of the ark with you' (Gen 9:10). Once again one can see God's concern for the whole of his fallen creation.

It was an amplification of the cultural mandate — the cultural mandate was not annulled by the Fall, nor even by the Flood, but was re-affirmed and even amplified. The stream of obligation is now increased through the movement of history.

One can see the three main aspects of the cultural mandate in the following passages:

marriage	Gen 1:28	(compare with Gen 9:1)
work	Gen 1:28	(compare with Gen 9:3)
government	Gen 1:29	(compare with Gen 9:2)

There are, however, two additional features: a food taboo, and a prohibition against murder. At this point God specifically gives animals as food for man, but there was a limit — that of eating meat with blood still in it (Gen 9:4). The fuller significance of blood, life, and atonement were to come clearer later. God also commands capital punishment for murder. The significance of this is that man is different from other animals. He is made in the image of God, and as such he is distinct from other animals. Even after the Fall man still retains something of God's image, and we must continue to remember the unique value of a human life. Every individual has a personality with feelings and aspirations, and is not a machine nor a part of the scenery. Christian mission must never lose sight of this point.

The covenant was given with a sign — the rainbow is a particularly appropriate symbol as it covers the whole of that to which it applies — man and the rest of creation (Gen 9:16).

Finally, the covenant will be everlasting between God and his whole creation. Not only did sinful men die in the Flood, but much of the animal and plant life as well. God's care for all of his creation will eventually lead to its final redemption as shown in Romans 8:19-23 with the Second Coming of Christ.

The mission of Noah and his descendants is involved with the fortunes of the Earth. In the midst of the failure of humankind, and the judgement of God, one can sense the mercy of God reaching out to his fallen creation. To Adam and Eve, as they hide in shame in the garden, God calls out, 'Where are you?' (Gen 3:9). Here is the beginning of the mission of God.

Discussion Questions

1 Niebuhr wrote, 'Because man has a capacity for justice, democracy is possible; because man has a capacity for injustice, democracy is necessary.' Discuss this statement in the light of the Fall.

2 How should the reality of the wrath of God affect the message of the Church to the world?

3 Although only Noah is described as being righteous before God, his obedience led to the salvation of his whole

family. Gather passages from the book of Acts where whole households believed and were baptised.

Recommended Reading
Ron Elsdon, *Bent World* (IVP: Leicester, 1981).

Footnotes

1   Excerpt from a drama by three players at Buloba College, Uganda, described in Eugene Nida, *Customs and Culture* (Harper & Brothers: New York, 1954) p 196.

2   R K Harrison *Introduction to the Old Testament* (Tyndale Press: London 1970) pp 454-461.

3   John Calvin *Commentaries on the Book of Genesis Vol I* (Calvin Translation Society: Edinburgh, 1847) p 125.

4   Louis Berkhof *Systematic Theology* (Banner of Truth Trust: London, 1959) pp 246-7.

5   R G V Tasker *New Bible Dictionary* IVP: Leicester, 1968) p 1341.

4

MULTI-CULTURAL MAN

A long, long time ago, say the Ashanti, God lived in the sky but close to men. One woman, who was pounding the national food (fufu) constantly, went on knocking against him with her long pestle. God decided therefore to go up higher. The woman advised her children to construct a tower of mortars piled one on top of another. This they did, and when they had used up all the mortars, there was only a short distance left, the length of one mortar. The woman instructed her children to take the bottom-most mortar in order to fill up the final gap. They did so, but the entire tower went tumbling down and killed many people. Those who survived gave up the attempt to reach God.[1]

From the family of Noah, who had been saved from the Flood, emerged a new society. As one would assume, and as Gensis chapters 9-11 state, the descendants of Noah had one language and one culture. How is it then that we are now faced with a world filled with many different languages and cultures? How is it that humankind became multi-cultural? These are the questions for this present chapter. In particular we will consider the aspects of language, civilisation, and religion, all of major importance in appreciating the context of mission in the twentieth century world.

Language

Genesis 11:1 reads: 'Now the whole world had one language and a common speech.' The passage stresses the fact that there was a common language and culture among the descendants of Noah. Genesis 10 is usually regarded by scholars as an ancient text which is used by the writer to

41

relate the descendants of Noah to the peoples of his own time. Thus, the fact that Genesis chapter 10 comes before chapter 11 is not significant with regard to the flow of the biblical narrative. What is significant is that each of the emerging tribes came to be 'each with its own language' (Gen 10:5, 20, 31).

The biblical account of this occurrence is the well known story of Babel. The word Babel is interesting in itself because it has two meanings: the Babylonians themselves used it to mean the 'Gate of God'; while to the Hebrews it meant 'confusion'. This play on the meaning of the word is to be found right through the Bible, even to the book of Revelation.

Most anthropologists hold to an evolutionary model for the development of cultures. They would argue that as *homo sapiens* evolved, possibly in more than one area though at about the same time, they developed various skills for providing for their basic needs and these became the rudiments of culture. Over a long period of time, and as a result of diffusion of ideas and skills between various groups, the wide variety of cultures known today was formed.

Although the Genesis account has been subject to various interpretations by biblical scholars, the text clearly indicates that the transformation of humankind from a mono-cultural to a multi-cultural society was the result of the direct intervention of God. The descendants of Noah showed the same inclination to sin as did their forefathers. They turned away from God and looked for their satisfaction and their personal and social fulfilment in collectivism and urbanisation (Gen 11:4). Fallen man had to be protected from himself and all that he could achieve for evil but at the same time given the opportunity to develop all his creative potential (Gen 11:6).

God acts in this situation. 'Come, let us go down and confuse their language so they will not understand each other' (Gen 11:7). The basic confusion among people is expressly stated as language, and not race or politics. The divisions among humankind are the result of sin and the specific form of judgement executed by God. The outcome is that yet another division comes to humankind. He now is separated socially from other groups by communication barriers.

The outcome was that the different language groups began to move away from Babel in various migrations. The table of the nations in Genesis chapter 10 is important in showing both the unity and diversity of humankind. Genesis 9:19 makes it quite clear that the entire human race as it now stands came from the three sons of Noah. Yet it is by the creative hand of God that the diversity of human cultures came into being.

However, within this act of judgement there is an element of hope. The fragmentation of humankind into a multicultural society gave numerous opportunities for at least one society to come into being which would be holy and God-seeking. G Steiner[2] said that there is a likelihood of there having been something between 8,000 and 10,000 languages in use throughout the history of man. Each language, in being the heart of a culture, gave man the freedom to dream, to invent, and to analyse in a multitude of different ways. Even so, Romans chapter 1 stresses the sad truth that all of humankind has sinned and is under the judgement of God.

The story of Babel is the story of a breakdown in human communication. It can only fully be understood in the light of what was to happen later at Pentecost, when unity was restored to mankind by the gift of tongues. At Pentecost, the Spirit of Love was given to men, to break down the barriers that separated Jew from Gentile, and one nation from another. All present heard the marvels of the Lord spoken in their own language (Acts 2:8-12).

It is necessary to realise that at Pentecost although unity was established, cultural uniformity was not restored. The unity of humankind is not restored by human organisation or education, but by unity with God and the indwelling of his Holy Spirit within the Body of his Church.

From the time of Babel, humankind is to be characterised by numerous ways of life within which each society seeks to cope with the world in which it lives. These cultures change to adapt to the environment and the needs of the society. The result is that humankind has become a vast cultural mosaic, each society showing the richness of human creativity, and also the degradation of which man is capable.

Civilisation

Not only does the story of the tower of Babel provide us with a symbol of human diversity, it may also provide us with a lesson on socio-economic development. The building of the tower was most probably associated with the technological development in the manufacturing of burnt bricks. The stronger bricks so produced would have allowed the construction of multi-storied buildings. Many scholars associate this tower with the ziggurats of Babylonia[3].

The story of God's judgement on the people does not mean that God is against development or urbanisation. Through the earlier passages of the Genesis account one can see the potential of human creativity. Jabal was a nomad with herds of domesticated animals (Gen 4:20). His brother Jubal was a musician, and Tubal-Cain made tools out of bronze and iron (Gen 4:22). The cultural mandate encouraged humankind to work and create from the surrounding environment. The covenant with Noah re-endorsed this, and we read of Noah cultivating the vine (Gen 9:20).

Divine punishment came because of the attitude of human pride displayed in the construction of the tower and the city. The people said, 'Come, let us build ourselves a city, with a tower that reaches to the heavens, so that we may make a name for ourselves and not be scattered over the face of the whole earth' (Gen 11:4). Thus Babel illustrates the idolatrous exaltation of human culture. It reveals the pride that man may have in his own accomplishments and technology. This ethnocentric pride which is common to all peoples can itself become a stumbling-block to the mission of the Church. As the missionary from a technologically developed culture goes to another with a less developed technology, it may be the technology he takes which makes the greatest impression on the people, not the religious message that he brings.

Religion

Religion is an important element within the worldview of any people. Different cultures would imply the possibility of different religious ideas. How the multiplicity of religions in the world came into being is a matter for debate. However, it is again essential to consider this subject if one is rightly to understand the nature of mission itself.

The Origin of Religion

E B Tylor,[4] Guy Swanson,[5] and other anthropologists have asserted that religion has evolved over the long history of humankind. Early *homo sapiens* formulated the notion of the soul and developed ideas about ghosts. These in turn lead to the postulation that the world is in fact full of spiritual forces. This worship of nature became expressed as a polytheistic religion, and it was only much later in man's evolution that humankind turned to monotheism. Archaeology does seem to reveal that early civilisations practised various forms of nature worship within a polytheistic system. However, such observations depend upon artefacts that have been discovered.

On the other hand, when one studies the first few chapters of Genesis, the religious practices described would have left no significant material artefacts. No priests or temples are mentioned, and the sacrifices offered, such as in Genesis 4 which tells the story of Abel offering an animal, and Cain presenting fruit, would have left little remains. Thus, there is nothing to hinder a proposal made by Robert Brown,[6] that before the existence of ancient civilisations investigated by archaeologists, man could have practised a form of religion similar to that described in the early chapters of Genesis.

According to Genesis the first religion of man was monotheism, but even in the first chapters one sees how humankind move from monotheism to polytheism, and not the reverse. Further evidence for monotheism amongst early man is found in the study of the history of Egypt. As Sir Wallis Budge has written, 'A study of ancient Egyptian religious texts will convince the reader that the Egyptians

45

believed in One God, who was self-existent, immortal, invisible, eternal . . . however far back we follow his literature, we never seem to approach a time when he was without this remarkable belief. It is true that he also developed polytheistic ideas and beliefs, and cultivated them at certain periods of his history'[7].

The belief in a supreme Creator God, amongst a host of lesser gods, is a concept common to many of the religions of Africa. However, for various reasons this supreme God has 'withdrawn' from them. This has left man preoccupied with a host of capricious spirits that also inhabit creation. Magic and sacred rituals are therefore used to fend off evil and to retain the harmony of nature. This required religious specialists who knew the rituals, and so across the world one saw a development of a priesthood with its temples and rituals. Robert Brown,[8] argues that in the sixth century BC there was a wave of revolt against the priesthood in many parts of the ancient world. In Persia there developed Zoroastrianism, while in India it was Buddhism and Jainism. In China, Confucianism and Taoism were widely accepted. It was at this time that a strong prophetic movement occurred in Israel seeking to take the people back from polytheism to monotheism.

Man is incurably religious, but his religion may quickly degenerate under the influence of his fantasies and fears. This pattern is to be seen on numerous occasions in the rest of the Old Testament, even among God's special people Israel. God sends his prophets to restore and re-establish true religion and worship.

The Problem of Other Religions

If one assumes that God revealed himself to Israel in a very particular way, what then was the origin of the other religions of the world? Many different answers have been given to this question, but they can be broadly grouped into three main classes.

First, there are those of the Christian tradition who have been impressed by the virtue and devotion found among

46

religions outside the Judeo-Christian tradition. E L Allan expresses this opinion in the following way: 'Heathenism is related to Christianity as law to gospel, reason to faith, nature to grace. The heathen is like a blind man, feeling the sun's warmth but not seeing the sun itself. Christ was within heathenism as natural potency but not yet as a personal principle.'[9]

This view was held in some Protestant missionary circles at the turn of the century, such as at the 1910 Edinburgh Conference.[6] However, this stance has largely been rejected because it has become obvious that different religions are not just seeking alternative answers to the same set of questions but are addressing themselves to totally different issues. One God is not just being worshipped by different names, but the whole concept of deity is totally different.

Other Christians regard all other religions as being from Satan. Emphasis is placed on the darker sides of other religions, and even that which may appear good is simply explained as the fact that Satan may manifest himself as an angel of light (II Cor 11:14). However, one must ask if it is right to assume that all that is apparently good in another religion is no more than a counterfeit of the goodness of God.

Yet others have seen these religions to be no more than human attempts to solve the primary issues of life, attempts to answer such questions as, 'Why am I here?', and 'What am I here for?' Some societies have been more successful than others in finding rational answers that enable them to live more successfully in the world.

All these models have their limitations; however, there is a fourth option which would seem to be more helpful, and this has been clearly presented by Sir Norman Anderson, who writes:

> The non-Christian religions seem to me to resemble a patchwork quilt, with brighter and darker components in differing proportions. There are elements of truth which must come from God himself, whether through the memory of an original revelation, through some process

47

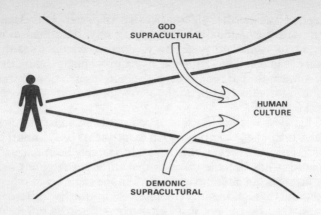

Fig 4:1

Influences on the Stream of Culture

of cross-fertilisation with some other religion, or through some measure of self-disclosure which, I cannot doubt, God still vouchsafes to those who truly seek him. But there are also elements which are definitely false, and which I, for one, believe come from 'the father of lies' — whose primary purpose is not so much to entice men into sensual sin as to keep them back, by any means in his power, from the only Saviour. Yet again, there is much that could best be described as human aspirations after the truth, rather than either divine revelation or Satanic deception.[10]

Figure 4:1 may be of use in picturing this viewpoint. Here the stream of human culture is seen as being influenced by God in his grace and sovereignty, and by Satan in his aim to resist God's purposes. A parallel may thus be seen between this model and that of the doctrine of total depravity. Here every part of human culture is seen as being affected by sin, but this does not mean that human culture is utterly depraved. Beauty and evil mix together in a wild confusion in every culture.

However we wish to read the biblical narrative of the tower of Babel, it is evident that humankind has developed into a scattering of peoples, each with their own language, customs and religion. Each nation had the opportunity of turning to God, but all failed. From the time of Babel this was to be the context in which the mission of God was to be accomplished.

Discussion Questions
1 What are your personal and national motives for desiring a higher standard of living?
2 Describe how one's view of the origin of other religions may affect one's attitude to the followers of those religions.
3 Take a good Bible commentary and explore the history of Babylon (Babel). The following passages will be of particular interest: Gen 11:1-9; Dan 4:29-37; Isa 13:17-22; Jer 51:41-49; Rev 17.

Recommended Reading
Robert Brown, *Religion – Origin and Ideas* (Tyndale: London, 1966).
Sir Norman Anderson, *Christianity and World Religions* (IVP: Leicester, 1984).
The World's Religions (Lion Handbook: Tring, 1982).

Footnotes
1   John S Mbiti, *Concepts of God in Africa* (SPCK: London, 1970) p 71.
2   George Stainer, 'After Babel', *The Listener* (April 1977): pp 510-514, 533-538.
3   R K Harrison, *Introduction to the Old Testament* (Tyndale Press: London, 1970) p 559.
4   E B Tylor, *Primitive Cultures* (John Murray: London, 1871).
5   Guy E Swanson, *The Birth of the Gods* (Ann Arbor Paperbacks: Michigan, 1968) pp 10-18.
6   Robert Brown, *Religion: Origins and Ideas* (Tyndale Press: London, 1966) pp 9-17.

7   E A Wallis Budge, *Egyptian Religion* (Routledge & Kegan Paul: London, 1899) pp 1-2.

8   Robert Brown, *op cit* pp 27-35.

9   E L Allan, *Christianity among the Religions* (SCM Press: London, 1960) p 70.

10   Sir Norman Anderson, *Christianity and World Religions* (IVP: Leicester, 1984) p 172.

5

THE CHOSEN PEOPLE

*I will make you a powerful and extensive community. I will be
with you and support you, so that you can support and strengthen
others. I will strengthen those who acknowledge and accept
strength, and he who refuses to have fellowship with you, who
turns away from you, who treats you with contempt, I will
abandon him and let him perish. Through you all the families of
the earth will find their true being and strength. In a word
through you will I fulfill the purpose of man's creation.[1]*

Genesis 1-11 is frequently known as universal history as it
deals with the whole of humankind. In Genesis 11:26 one
comes to a new situation in which God begins to deal with
one man in a particular and specific way. Abraham is a
person who can be placed in a particular historical and
cultural context. The Bible states that he originated from Ur
of the Chaldees.

Much is known about Ur because of the excavations that
were done by Sir Charles Woolley.[2] The history and economy of Ur is well known from thousands of inscribed tablets
and many buildings found at the site. They were a people of
a culture and civilisation that were advanced for that era.
They built two-storey houses with many rooms, plumbing
and sanitation systems, as well as pottery and many household items. They had a system of laws and administration in
advance of other peoples. The principal deity was Nannar
who was also worshipped as far away as Haran.

The biblical description of the lifestyle of the patriarchal
society agrees closely with that found from archaeological
evidence. It seems as though Abraham migrated from Ur

during the early part of the nineteenth century BC, and with that migration commenced a new and special work of God within human history.

The Call of Abraham

One cannot approach the subject of evangelism without confronting the subject of election. Why did God choose Abraham of all people? The Scriptures continually stress the fact that God *chose* Abraham, and through him the people of Israel. 'Long ago your forefathers, including Terah the father of Abraham and Nahor, lived beyond the River and worshipped other gods. But I took your father Abraham from the land beyond the River and led him throughout Canaan' (Josh 24:2, 3).

The Hebrew word for election, *bahar*, has two important connotations. The first is that of making a careful choice occasioned by actual needs. Secondly, *bahar* implied a special purpose or mission. The importance of the word is stressed by the fact that the verb alone occurs 164 times in the Old Testament. The word eventually became a technical term for the special act of God in calling out a person or a people from the rest of humankind for a particular task[3]. Three aspects can be seen in the election of Abraham.

The Call

God took the initiative. It was not the result of an earnest seeking by Abraham, but of God breaking into space and time to reveal himself. Here is one of the great principles of the Old Testament, that of God revealing himself to humankind in order to bring truth where there was confusion. The God who reveals himself to Abraham is later the same one who reveals himself to Isaac and Jacob, and then to Moses as the 'I am who I am' (Exod 3:6-17). It is through the patriarchs and the prophets that Yahweh was to reveal himself in a particular way, and through them to the descendants of Abraham — the people of Israel.

Abraham was not chosen because of some special merit on his part. It was not a matter of favouritism, but the active choice of God for some special service. The great sin of

Israel was later the belief that because they were chosen, they were God's favourites, and therefore superior to other nations. As Blauw expresses it: '. . . election is not primarily a privilege but a responsibility. If the responsibility is refused, election can even become a motive for divine punishment.'[4]

God required the separation of Abraham in order for him to fulfil that mission. Ur of the Chaldees was an area in which idolatry was practised, as has been testified by both archeology and Scripture (Josh 24:2). If God's new purpose was to be fulfilled, Abraham was required to separate himself from his homeland and move to a foreign region. Obedience was required as an outward demonstration of his faith (Heb 11:8-10).

The Covenant

Three things characterise the promise that God made to Abraham: First, he promised to make the descendants of Abraham into a great nation. For a man to be the founder of a tribe was the greatest honour of the ancient world. His impact on world history would continue now far beyond his death, and his name would be remembered for ever by that people. In making this promise, God showed his plan of raising up a new people who would in a special way be his people. Through this nation God was about to fulfil his plan of redemption. At this point the theme of the people of God acquires a new and fuller meaning that will span the Bible until it reaches its climax in the book of Revelation.

Secondly, God promised Abraham a new country. The people would need a land in which to live and provide for their physical needs, a land in which a society could develop so as to fulfil the cultural mandate. It would thus demonstrate the way in which God would have man live.

The land that God promised to Abraham and his descendants was to be of strategic importance. It bordered on the Mediterranean Sea, which was to become the heart of the sea trade of the ancient world. Through the land of Israel would pass two of the great trade routes of the world; one road crossing from Asia to Egypt, and the second from

Europe heading to Arabia in the south. In this way the people of Israel would be the focus of a worldwide influence.

Thirdly, God promised a blessing: 'I will make you into a great nation and I will bless you. I will make your name great and you will be a blessing' (Gen 12:2). Not only are Abraham and his people to be recipients of a blessing, but that blessing will in turn come to all peoples because of Israel. The promise of God's blessing provides Israel with the necessary resources to accomplish the purposes of God as his people. This blessing was not given to Israel for itself alone, but in order that the blessing of God might reach out to all peoples. In the very heart of God's selection of this one people, the universal concern for all humankind is still central.

The Commission

Unlike the covenant with Noah, this covenant includes conditions for both parties. Many scholars have mentioned the fact that the form of the Old Testament covenants are similar to the classical treaties of that period. In both the treaties and the covenants one sees the undeserved favour of the overlord together with the expectations required of the vassal[5]. Central to the covenant with Abraham was the sign of circumcision (Gen 17: 9-14). Circumcision would show that there was a special agreement between the descendants of Abraham and God. If any male was not circumcised, God would no longer consider him one of his chosen people. Circumcision was therefore to become an essential feature of Hebrew religion, and the worship of Yahweh was to become the focus of their life and culture.

The story of the patriarchs is a story of the progressive de-culturalisation of polytheistic elements and lifestyle in the light of divine disclosure. God was going to reveal himself in the culture of this his special people. These people were to show something of the character and nature of God in their very culture, so that the supra-cultural would be revealed within the Hebrew culture.

The Nations

How is it that God by selecting a people will bring universal blessing to all peoples? God wanted to reveal his nature through human form so that others could come to know him. The election of Israel did not mean the rejection of the other nations. God, in focussing his particular attention upon one people, in no way loses his concern for all peoples. It is through Israel that God will accomplish his purpose, which will bring blessing to all nations.

In today's thinking, a 'nation' is a socio-political state, but this is not what is understood by the Hebrew term *goyyim*, usually translated 'nation'. The *goyyim* were people with their own cultural and linguistic identity, but — what is more — they had their own religious system. Their gods were tribal gods, and the surrounding nations frequently looked upon Yahweh as no more than the tribal god of Israel. At times, even Israel herself fell into the trap, considering Yahweh to be its national god.

The Nations as Judgement

From Genesis chapter 12 onwards, the other nations are always considered with respect to their relationship to Israel. There is no uniform judgement on the nations, but it is always based on their practical relationship with and attitude towards Israel. Genesis 12:3, 'I will bless those who bless you, and whoever curses you I will curse.' Here cursing and blessing are to be seen in redemptive terms.

On this basis, foreign nations were regarded as either the rightful spoil of Israel or as the instruments of God's chastening of his people. The Canaanites were driven out of the land because of their wickedness (Deut 9:4, 5). Israel was required to wait four generations in Egypt, 'for the sin of the Amorites has not yet reached its full measure' (Gen 15:16). God's justice is central to his dealings with the nations.

On the other hand, whenever Israel turns away from God and becomes linked with other nations and their gods, it loses its right of existence as the people of God. God then uses these very nations as the instruments of his judgement on Israel.

The Nations as Witnesses

God's dealings with Israel did not occur in isolation but were witnessed by the nations. As the Psalmist writes:

God, be merciful to us and bless us;

look on us with kindness,

so that the whole world may know your will;

so that all nations may know your salvation.

Ps 67:1, 2

The nations are witnesses to the character of God both seen within the lifestyle of God's people, and through God's dealing with them. In the Old Testament one does not find the out-going thrust of missionaries who cross frontiers to pass on their message, but one does find the attraction of individuals to the nation of Israel itself.

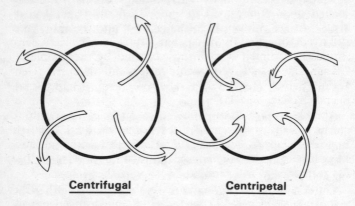

Centrifugal   **Centripetal**

Fig 5:1

The Nation As Witnesses

Blauw[6] and others have spoken of these aspects by the terms 'centripetal' and 'centrifugal' (see figure 5:1). The centripetal represents a drawing to the centre in the same way as a magnet draws iron filings to itself. One sees examples of this with Ruth, and the Queen of Sheba, both of whom are impressed by Israel and so are drawn to her.

Centrifugal mission, on the other hand, is a flinging out into an active missionary task. In this respect, the little story of Jonah stands alone in the Old Testament. However, when one arrives at the New Testament a new dimension emerges, and the commission is given to go to all peoples.

The Patriarchs and Their Cultures

Genesis chapters 12-50 reveal the rooting of God's purposes in four generations of patriarchs and the associated growth of a family into a tribe. It also shows how these people lived in two very different cultures: the nomadic life in Canaan, and the settled agriculture in Egypt. Various references are made to their way of life and how this fulfilled the cultural mandate.

The conversion of Abraham from his traditional religion to that of worshipping Yahweh did not mean a distinct break with his culture. In the majority of his ways Abraham still lived according to the customs of his people. He set up shrines in a similar way to those erected by the people of Canaan. He established 'sacred places' at Shechem (Gen 12:6), Bethel (Gen 12:8), Hebron (Gen 13:18), and Beersheba (Gen 21:33).

Abraham still continued to follow many of the cultural norms of his day, which often leaves the twentieth century Bible expositor in confusion. The apparent willingness to allow his wife to be taken by the King of Egypt (Gen 12:10-20) seems to be so contradictory to what has happened in the first part of the chapter with the call of God. The practice of polygamy and the taking of concubines were all part of the culture of that period. Even so, one begins to see God at work within the patriarchs and their families, one example being through the rebuffs of pagan kings (Gen 12:18, 19).

The patriarchs sought to obey the laws of the land and conform to the local customs. One instance of this is the purchase of a burial place for Sarah by Abraham (Gen 23:4-20). That they sought to live peaceably with others is illustrated with the story of Isaac and the wells (Gen 26:15-22). However, they disassociated themselves from the surrounding Canaanites in two very important ways: First, they disapproved of marrying Canaanite women (Gen 24:3, 28:3). If the family line was to remain pure, Isaac could not marry a Canaanite woman, but only one from his own family. As the family became a people they remained endogenous — they grew solely from within — and so retained their distinct identity.

Secondly, they disassociated themselves from flagrant immorality. The destruction of Sodom (Gen 19), the rape of Dinah (Gen 34), and the attempted seduction of Joseph (Gen 39) all illustrate the growing distinctiveness of the Hebrews as a people.

Joseph is a remarkable illustration of a man who was both a servant of God and also a servant of Pharoah. His promotion was unsought, although he displayed no hesitation in accepting political responsibility. He devoted his energy and wisdom to promoting Egypt's interests, and therefore those of his own people who were caught up with the host nation. He demonstrates the possibility of being equally a servant of God and a worker for Pharoah.

Israel was to become the centre of God's redemptive purposes for humankind, to be the people of God — and so a witness to all. This was to be the mission of Israel to the nations. God committed himself to Israel in a special way, and his promises to them become clearer in the great act of the Exodus.

Discussion Questions

1 What issues are raised by the lifestyle of the patriarchs for Christians living as a religious minority within a pluralistic society?

2 How does the call of Abraham show that history is more than a random flow of events?

3 Study the life of Joseph to see how he was able to be both the servant of Pharoah and faithful to God. How may these principles be applied by a Christian living in a secular society?

Recommended Reading

John R W Stott, 'The Living God is a Missionary God' in *Perspectives on the World Christian Movement — a reader* (William Carey Library: Pasadena, 1981) pp 10-18.

J Jeremias, *Jesus' Promise to the Nations* (SCM Press: London, 1958).

Oswald Chambers, *Not Knowing Whither* (Marshall Ltd: Basingstoke, 1949).

Footnotes

1   Philip Potter in Richard R DeRidder, *Discipling the Nations* (Baker Book House: Grand Rapids, 1975) p 25.

2   R K Harrison, *Introduction to the Old Testament* (Tyndale Press: London, 1970) pp 99-105.

3   Donald Senior, and Carroll Stuhlumueleer, *The Biblical Foundations for Mission* (SCM Press: London, 1983) pp 94-98.

4   Johannes Blauw, *The Missionary Nature of the Church* (Lutterworth Press: London, 1962) p 23.

5   'Covenants & Near Eastern Treaties' *The Lion Handbook to the Bible* (Lion Publishing: Tring, 1973: pp 198-199.

6   Johannes Blauw, *op cit*, p 34.

6

CRY, FREEDOM

If the world was a village of 1,000 people there would be 60 North Americans, 80 South Americans, 210 Europeans, 544 Asians (and 106 Africans).

If the world was a village of 1,000 people there would be 700 coloured persons and 300 whites, and also 300 Christians.

If the world was a village of 1,000 people, 60 people would own half of the total income, 500 would go hungry to bed, 600 would live in the slums, 700 would be illiterate!

If this be our village we should surely try to change this. But it is, in fact our village, since it is our world![1]

The book of Exodus relates the story of the great event of salvation in the Old Testament. It is one of the most dramatic deliverances of an oppressed people in all of history, and the Hebrew people were to look back to that event as crucial to their becoming a nation.

Land of Oppression

The story of the migration of the descendants of Abraham to Egypt, due to the famine in Canaan, is well known. Initially, this nomadic family was welcomed by the Egyptians because they realised how Joseph had helped them prepare for the famine. With time, memories of Joseph faded, and a new Pharoah came to power who began to oppress and exploit the Hebrews. This oppression illustrates so many of the factors one finds among other exploited peoples down through the history of the world, still existing today.

Prejudice

For centuries the Hebrews had lived in the land of Egypt, and throughout that time they had kept themselves as a distinct ethnic group. The Hebrews were Semitic people who would have been lighter skinned than the Egyptians, who were Hamites.

The Hebrews were also culturally different from the Egyptians. They were pastoral nomads whose life centred around the care of their animals. They ate different foods from the Egyptians, had different patterns of work, and probably even smelt different. The Egyptian dislike of the nomadic shepherds is probably no different to the feelings most settled people today have towards such wanderers. As a result they allowed the Hebrews to settle in one particular area and so retain their particular identity (Gen 46:34). As is common in many areas of the world where nomadic herders live near settled farmers, tensions occur which can often explode into violence.

Minorities
The Hebrews were a minority in the country, and as in many societies minorities easily become the focus of exploitation. Prejudice brings with it fear, and fear leads to exploitation of the minority groups (Exod 1:9, 10). The Hebrews were used as slave labour by the Egyptians to build their new cities.

The story goes on to illustrate one of the paradoxes of poverty. It is the poor who increase in numbers more than the rich (Exod 1:12). The poor work the hardest for the least reward and yet multiply more than others — as we see today. Although it is popularly considered that the poor are poor because they have many children, in fact the reverse is true. Poor people have many children because they need their children to look after them when they are old. They do not have material goods on which they can depend and so must look to their children for future support.

Oppression always stems from a distorted view of people. Pharoah saw the Hebrews merely as 'production units' for his use. Whenever the intrinsic worth of the individual human being is lost, discrimination and oppression occur. This is why the Christian Church must have a right understanding of the nature of man. Even though he is fallen, he

61

still bears something of the nature of God. Thus, whatever his race or culture all men have intrinsic value, and no man is of less worth than another: 'Rich and poor have this in common: the Lord is the Maker of them all' (Prov 22:2); 'He who mocks the poor shows contempt for their Maker' (Prov 17:5).

Revolt

Such a situation of oppression is ripe for revolution. The Hebrew midwives disobeyed Pharoah's command to kill any male babies born (Exod 1:16, 17). These women were willing to put their lives at risk because they recognised a higher law than that decreed by man — the moral law of God. Today, oppressed people may organise a protest march, a strike, hold a conference, or allow their frustrations to explode into mob violence. The Bible does not tell us if any of these options were even possible for the Hebrews, but it does say, 'Their cry for help because of their slavery went up to God' (Exod 2:23).

The Struggle for Justice

'So God looked on the Israelites and was concerned about them' (Exod 2:25). God cares about social injustice. He cares when people are hurting. His cry is 'Let my people go . . .'

An essential question currently debated is how this liberation is to be accomplished. Should violence be used to achieve God's purposes? How was this question to be worked out for the Israelites in Egypt? Harvey Perkins responds to this question: 'We have given our message the title, "Let my people go." Let us explain why. With this cry, Moses demanded that His people be released from slavery, "Let go" is a call for liberation. From that time on, liberation has been the central theme of God's redeeming work.'[2]

Moses — God's Man

Modern knowledge of Egypt yields a rich background to the early life of Moses. He was adopted into one of the harems to be found along the Nile during the period of the New Kingdom (1570-1085 BC). There he was educated and no doubt rose to a position of some authority.

Moses was a man with a social conscience and a heart that felt for the underprivileged. He was also a violent and passionate man, and on two occasions expressed his concern in direct action. First, on seeing an Egyptian beating an Israelite, he sprang to the man's defence and killed the guard (Exod 2:11-16). When this act became known Moses had to flee for his life. And on the second occasion, Moses helped Jethro's daughters in the land of Midian when the local shepherds tried to drive them away (Exod 2:16-19).

His first attempt to right the wrongs of the underprivileged was unplanned and misguided. He made a move for justice, but he acted in a way that was high-handed and so compromised himself. Moses' recourse to violent action did not liberate the Hebrews, but — later — it did protect Jethro's daughters. While it is right to have strong feelings about social injustice, immediate action is not always the most effective way to right the wrong.

Liberation Achieved

H H Rowley has called Moses 'the first missionary.'[3] He was called by God to lead the people of God out of captivity that they might worship Him (Exod 3:7-12). How was this accomplished?

First, the 40 years in the wilderness clearly had a profound effect upon Moses. Much of the self-confidence which characterised his earlier years was gone, and one finds a much meeker man — a man better able to accomplish the deliverance of Israel under God.

The experience of the burning bush was essential for Moses. Here God revealed himself by a new name of Yahweh, the 'I AM' (the Lord) — Exod 3:14. The message of Moses to the people of Israel was that a deity by the name of Yahweh, the same as who had appeared to their ancestors, would be instrumental in bringing them out of captivity in Egypt. In the Exodus, Israel was going to come to know God, above everything else, as a God of salvation. He was the one who delivered them from bondage and brought them out into a promised land. Time and time again the later prophets of Israel were to point the people back to the God who acted in history to bring liberation to his people.

This deliverance was accomplished by the supernatural intervention of God. The gods of Egypt were often embodiments of natural forces or phenomena, such as the sun and the moon.[4] Pharoah himself was regarded as divine, being a link between the gods and man. The great temples maintained the official cults with all their spectacular priesthood and worship. Ordinary people had their household gods. Magic was common for healing and performing miracles. It was believed that by calling on the name of the appropriate god in the right way, one could accomplish many varied miraculous acts. The biblical record does not deny this and describes how, when Moses casts his rod on the floor and it changed into a snake, the magicians did likewise (Exod 7:8-13).

The plagues present a remarkable demonstration of the power of God to move into space and time, and to accomplish the miraculous. It is to be noted that each of the first nine plagues has a direct bearing on the gods of Egypt. The Egyptian gods were related to nature spirits which held great influence over the prosperity of the nation as a whole. Ha'pi, the Nile god, had to be appeased because he brought prosperity; frogs were the symbol of Heqit, a goddess of fruitfulness; Ra was the sun-god. But each of the nine plagues directly confronted the gods of Egypt and showed Yahweh to be greater. This point could not have been missed by either the Hebrews or the Egyptians.

Yahweh demonstrated his full control over the forces of nature, and therefore over the gods in which the Egyptians believed. Yahweh speaks of executing judgement against the gods of Egypt. 'On that same night I will pass through Egypt and strike down every first-born – both men and animals – and I will bring judgement on all the gods of Egypt' (Exod 12:12). Even Pharoah, the god-king on earth, was to suffer. God is One who acts within history to accomplish his purposes. This truth is to be a focal issue for the people of God throughout history, and an issue that the Church of our age needs to realise.

Thus, not only were the Israelites to come to know Yahweh — the Liberator — but the Egyptians were also to come forcibly to know of Israel's God. In the power struggle between Pharoah and God, Pharoah at first cries, 'Who is the Lord? . . . I do not know the Lord' (Exod 5:2). Repeatedly in the narrative God makes it clear that it is his intention that the Egyptians come to know about him, and to realise that there is none like him (Exod 7:5, 17; 9:14, 29). The climax of the encounter comes when the Egyptian army is finally destroyed in the swirling waters (Exod 14:18).

The missionary aspect is not concealed. Whatever else the Egyptians were to comprehend, they must have come to realise the power Yahweh had exercised on behalf of their former slaves. The Egyptians did not come to faith in Yahweh, but they had been confronted with his power and majesty and had witnessed a God who acts in history.

On one occasion, Moses asked God not to destroy the complaining Israelites because of the negative effect that this would have on what the Egyptians had witnessed (Num 14:13-16). God was planning that the nations might see what he is like through his dealings with his people.

Liberation Theology

In recent years, the Exodus account has been given a central role in a particular view of mission which has become commonly known as liberation theology. It was in 1959 that Ernst Bloch wrote his major work *Theology of Hope*.[5] Bloch argued that the Christian hope is not just something vague and in the future but has a reality which is immediate and political. This idea has been taken up by many Latin American theologians and has been stimulated by a growing interaction with Marxist teaching. Today there are many schools of thought within the movement, but one can identify several common features.

Outline of Liberation Teaching

Liberation theology is considered not to be just an alternative set of ideas concerning the teaching of the Bible, but a new way of looking at theology. Traditional theology, it is claimed, is an abstract presentation of the truths of revelation, and practical action had to be deduced from this foundation. Liberation theology, on the other hand, starts with the social situation of the period, and more specifically the situation of poverty experienced by many in Latin America. The Christian should accordingly be committed to act on behalf of the poor, and it is from this position that the Christian should view his theology. Even salvation is considered in terms of liberation. The way of dividing history into the 'sacred' and the 'secular' is considered to be wrong, because God is woking out salvation in all of human history. Within history the Church must be God's sign of salvation in the world.

The Church in its mission must therefore be prepared to take a positive stance with regard to the poor and the exploited. To profess a political neutrality is in fact to support the status quo. For centuries the Roman Catholic Church in Latin America has been allied with the rich land owners, but this — it is claimed — must now cease. Liberation theology has been embraced by many priests working among the poor of Latin America who have endeavoured to increase the lot of the poor, even though it means conflict with the rich.

Liberation theologians also see oppression in the domination of Western ideas and practice. Liberation is to be sought politically, economically, and culturally. This, they argue, is what happened with the Exodus, and a similar liberation is advocated for the poor and oppressed of today.

A New Approach to Mission?

It is all too easy for those from a traditional school of theological thought to brush aside what is being said by the liberation theologians without listening to what they are actually saying. They are concerned with the oppression of the poor by the rich, frequently a concern that the Christian

66

Church has ignored. But the Exodus reveals to us that God is concerned about the poor and the oppressed, and those of us from the rich Western world must ask ourselves whether we are equally concerned about the poor.

Although one may appreciate the sympathies of the liberation theologians towards the poor, and understand the compelling attractiveness of liberation theology for many in a suffering world, it is necessary to realise that Jesus bypassed the revolutionary option. On several occasions the crowd would have taken him and by force established him as King of the Jews. Each time Christ avoided the possibility. He knew that he had come with an even more radical message, to set men free from the greater bondage of sin. Even so, the people of God must not be complacent about their responsibility to cry justice when the poor are being exploited.

A study of the history of the Church shows many incidents when the Church has sought to obtain justice through the use of violence, Oliver Cromwell's massacre of the Irish being a case in point. Broadly speaking it may be said that on those occasions the very same Christian sentiment which in the first place prompted the defence of the poor, is eventually crowded out; spirituality itself is finally totally abandoned. All too often liberation is conceived of as being the end in itself. In contrast, Exodus shows that after liberating Israel God takes them on to Sinai. He does so for the higher purpose of making them his people: 'I will take you as my own people, and I will be your God' (Exod 6:7).

Discussion Questions

1 What aspects of racial or cultural prejudice do you know of that occur in your society?

2 Is there a time when violence is the only option open to a Christian?

3 Do you agree that the Bible must take priority over social and political theories in determining Christian belief and action? If so, how can one avoid the division between the sacred and the secular?

Recommended Reading

Andrew J Kirk, *Liberation Theology* (Marshalls Theological Library: Basingstoke, 1979).

Ronald Sider, *Christ and Violence* (Lion Publishing:Tring, 1980).

Footnotes

1   Quoted by Rob Bellingham *A Biblical Basis for Development* (HEED: Bangladesh, 1982) p 4.

2   Harvey Perkins, 'Let My People Go', *Mission Trends No 3: Third World Theologies* (Eerdmans: Grand Rapids, 1976) p 193.

3   H H Rowley, *Israel's Mission to the World* (SCM Press: London, 1939).

4   See Wallis E A Budge, *Egyptian Religion* (Routledge & Kegan Paul: London, 1899).

5   Ernest Bloch, *Man On His Own* (Herder & Herder: New York, 1970).

7

HOW SHOULD THEY THEN LIVE?

Back before they (the Bahinemo) had had Christian teaching, I tried to translate Jesus' list of sins in Mark 7. As each sin was described, they gave me the local term for it. They named other sins in their culture.

'What did your ancestors tell you about these things?' I asked them.

'Oh, they told us we shouldn't do any of those things.'

'Do you think they were good standards that your ancestors gave you?' They agreed unanimously that they were.

'Well, do you keep all these rules?'

'No,' they responded sheepishly.

One leader said, 'Definitely not. Who could ever keep them all? We're people of the ground.'

I took this opportunity to explain that God expected them to keep their own standards for what is right, that He was angry because they hadn't. Then I pointed out that it was because they fell short of their own standards that God sent His son to bear their punishment so they could be reunited with Him.

This was a crucial step towards their conversion. For the first time the Scriptures were linked to what God was telling them through their consciences. Within a year, most of the people in that village had committed themselves to Christ.[1]

Birth of a Nation

Peoples of antiquity dated their beginnings from some specific act. For the Romans it was the initiation of the building of the city of Rome. For the Greeks it was the inauguration of their first communal games. For the Israelites it was the Exodus.

The Israelites were led out of Egypt to Sinai, where God presented to them the offer of a covenant relationship. The pivotal statement consists of a promise: 'you will be my treasured possession', and a demand, 'you will be for me a kingdom of priests.' In doing this the Israelites entered into a solemn commitment of themselves to the God who had delivered them. Election demands the response of worship and service (Exod 19:3-9). What was it to mean for Israel to be the people of God?

First, they were to be a community with a particular sense of solidarity built around the covenant. As such they would have the opportunity to construct and develop their own culture. In Egypt, they had few options as to the lifestyle they would follow, but now as a nation they would have the opportunity to build a new way of life.

They were also to be the people of a specific God — Yahweh — around whom their worship would centre. The God who had redeemed them had the right to possess them. Although the first commandment does not deny the possibility of other 'gods', it does demand that Israel was to worship only one God — the Lord. The elaborate ritual enabled the devout to experience a dynamic interaction with Yahweh that brought assurance of forgiveness and acceptance. From henceforth, Israel was to, 'fill a priestly role as a people in the midst of peoples: she represents God in the world of nations. What priests are for a people, Israel as a people is for the world.'[2]

Israel was to be a people of the Law. It is popularly thought that Israel had to obey the Law in order to be saved, but Exodus 20 is given to a people who have *already* been chosen and delivered. The Law was given not to establish a close relationship, but to perpetuate it. The relationship with God had commenced in Egypt, but in the Law had the means of expressing and maintaining that relationship.

Life of a Nation

God wanted his people to live a lifestyle which revealed his character. This did not just relate to certain religious practices and beliefs, but to their whole way of life. The division between the sacred and the secular which so dominates our Western thinking is not found in Israelite society. Within the book of Exodus one finds an integrated whole in which religious law mixes easily with social behaviour. Following the giving of the Ten Commandments in Exodus 20 comes the treatment of slaves in chapter 21, then laws relating to theft. Chapter 23 is about justice, after which comes the institution of the three great festivals (Exod 23:14-19), and in chapter 24 the covenant is sealed. The Law reflected the lifestyle God wanted Israel to adopt.

This lifestyle may best be described by the Hebrew word *shalom*. Although this word is usually translated into English by the word 'peace', it has a far wider and richer meaning than just the absence of disturbance which is associated with the word peace. Richardson defines *shalom* as follows:

> *Shalom* is a comprehensive word, covering the manifold relationships of daily life, and expressing the ideal state of life in Israel. Fundamental meaning is 'totality', 'wholeness', 'well-being', 'harmony', with stress on material prosperity untouched by violence or misfortune.[3]

Shalom speaks of all the positive features which should characterise the culture of the people of God. *Shalom* amplifies the cultural mandate and broadens still further the 'stream of obligation'. In this case the mandate refers particularly to the Hebrew people, because they — in a very particular way — are to reveal the purposes of God to the nations.

By witnessing Yahweh's presence and activity in Israel, the nations are summoned to recognise him as the God of the whole earth. As Blauw says of Israel 'She represents God in the world of nations.'[4] In practice, sinful Israel herself needed this *shalom*, and it would remain for the suffering servant to fulfil this task.

71

The particular culture proposed by the covenant with Israel provides us with a demonstration of the sort of life he wants man to live. Out of all the various cultures that already existed, none was pleasing to God, but here in God's plan for Israel was one pattern by which a society might please God and remain in fellowship with him.

The Land

'Leviticus 25 is one of the most radical texts in all of Scripture. At least it seems that way for people born in countries committed to a laissez-faire economics.'[4] Thus writes Ronald Sider.

The land belongs, not to man, but to God. This is a totally different concept from that found in Western societies where land can be bought and sold, and used or abused as the owner desires. In Israel, a man was not to think of himself as an owner of the land, but as a responsible tenant: 'The land must not be sold permanently, because the land is mine and you are but aliens and my tenants' (Lev 25:23).

This concept of the land and the role of man as the responsible tenant is much closer to that given in the cultural mandate than that followed by Western society today. For the Hebrews this had some marked repercussions as to how they were to deal with the land.

In the first place, the people were God's tenants and as such were required to pay a rent. However, this was not to be a rent to a rich landlord living at ease in a castle, but to those of God's people who had no land. 'At the end of every three years, bring all the tithes of that year's produce and store it in your towns, so that the Levites (who have no allotment or inheritance of their own) and the aliens, the fatherless, and widows who live in your towns may come and eat and be satisfied, and so that the Lord your God may bless you in all the work of your hands' (Deut 14:28-29; see also Lev 27:30-32, Num 18:21-32).

In addition, the land was to be allowed to rest every seven years (Lev 25:2). In other words, the Israelites were not to practise intensive agriculture in which the good land was to be worked until it became a dust-bowl. It was God's creation, and the people as responsible tenants had to treat it as such. The *shalom* must include a realistic appreciation for ecology. In the fiftieth year the land was not only to be allowed to lie fallow, but it had to be restored to its original owners. 'It shall be a jubilee for you; each one of you is to return his family property and each to his own clan' (Lev 25:10). This principle was to have a radical effect on the whole culture of the Israelite peoples, though it was rarely actually applied.

The land was allocated according to tribes and families. The Hebrew family consisted of a large patriarchal household consisting of an extended family with at least three generations. Each tribe had its own area of land which was divided equally according to the size of the tribe (Num 26:52-56). The family was an important social and economic unit. Thus the practice of careful land stewardship would stop the permanent economic collapse of families through poverty and debt. The poverty of the previous generation would not come upon the younger generation as a total burden which would trap them into a life of poverty. As such it was an attempt to halt the relentless economic forces in society whereby the rich get richer and the poor get poorer. It would also stop the development of a land-owning aristocracy. The curse in many areas of the world today is that the land is owned by a few for whom the poor must work for meagre rewards. The 'jubilee' principle would mean that the Hebrew society would essentially be classless.

For Slaves: Justice

The Old Testament accepts the practice of slavery. However, the practice in the Middle East was different from that practised by the Romans and commonly understood as slavery by Western people today. For some of the Romans, slaves were no more than machines to be used as the master wished; they had few rights. In the Middle East slaves did have rights and could even have privileged places in a family. With the *shalom* lifestyle one sees a much more humane approach to slaves than found in any of the other societies of that day.

73

The law sought to avoid wholesale population drift into slavery through economic hardship. A Hebrew man who sold himself into slavery to escape poverty had to be released in the seventh year (Deut 15:12). Even as slaves they were to be regarded as part of the people of God. They were not to be regarded as inferior (Deut 15:15). They were to be protected (Exod 21:2-27; Lev 25:25-55). They were also to share in the religious festivals (Deut 16:11).

Unlike Hebrew slaves, foreign slaves could be enslaved for life and handed on with family inheritance. Though this was not true among the Israelites, even so they were encouraged to 'Remember that you were slaves in Egypt and the Lord your God redeemed you' (Deut 15:15). Here one sees a respect for all people, and for the God who created all humankind. However, the sad fact of Hebrew history is that the rich did not want to let their slaves go. This is illustrated by the sorry story in Jeremiah 34:8-22. In this case the people first agreed to free their slaves, but later changed their minds, took them back, and forced them to become slaves again.

For the Needy: Care

Mutual helpfulness was to characterise the people of God. The *shalom* culture recognised that with time some people may become poor for various reasons, many of which would be beyond the person's control. The rich should not use this opportunity to exploit the poor and make a profit for themselves by charging interest (Exod 22:25). Everyone must treat his fellow Israelite as a person, showing him compassion: 'If you take your neighbour's cloak as a pledge, return it to him by sun set, because his cloak is the only covering he has for his body' (Exod 22:26).

Widows and orphans, because they were helpless and so open to exploitation, were to be the subjects of special concern (Exod 22:22-24). Hebrew society was to be concerned about the weak ensuring that they were treated with justice and care. God himself will make them the subjects of his special concern (Ps 68:5, 6; Prov 15:25). In general, God wanted his people to have a simple lifestyle without materialism at its heart; the perils of both affluence and poverty were to be avoided.

For Immigrants: Protection

Previously Israel had lived as migrants in the land of Egypt; but as Israel was now going to be a nation in its own right, it would have responsibilities towards the foreigners who placed themselves under Israel's protection. The foreigners (*ger* in Hebrew, or *gerim* − plural) were to be treated in the same way as other Hebrews. 'When an alien lives with you in your land, do not ill-treat him. The alien living with you must be treated as one of your native-born. Love him as yourself, for you were aliens in Egypt' (Lev 19:33-34).

This would ensure that the *ger* would have the same legal status, the same laws of morality and ceremonial, applied to them as to the Israelites. Unchastity is forbidden (Lev 18:29), and idolatry condemned (Lev 20:2). The *ger* were not to be oppressed by the Israelites who were the majority people (Exod 22:21; 23:19). There was to be no discrimination against those who were not of Israel. When the foreigner accepted the full responsibilities of Israel's faith, he was in every respect an Israelite with all the same responsibilities and privileges as a native-born Israelite. Here was an open door by which the nations might become part of the people of God.

The Monarchy

The social structure assumed in the early centuries of Israel's history in the promised land was focussed upon the extended family, in which a patriarch was effectively the head of each family. The extended family then linked into the wider association of clans and the whole tribe. This form of structure assumes a basic theocracy. The rise of the monarchy proved to be one of the major political forces in the history of Israel.

A Man-made Institution

One thing that stands out clearly in the emergence of the monarchy is that this was not a divinely given institution, and this resulted in a long-standing antipathy towards kingship. This shows itself with Gideon's refusal, and horror, at the thought of being made king. 'I will not rule over you, nor will my son rule over you. The Lord will rule over you' (Judges 8:23).

The political crises described in the early chapter of I Samuel, when the Philistines were invading the land, made Israel cry out for a king. Israel was not able to trust God to deliver them, and preferred a man whom they could see. 'Now appoint a king who would lead us, such as all the other nations have' (I Sam 8:5). This demand angered Samuel, but as the Lord says to him in verse 7, 'it is not you that they have rejected as king, but me.'

The repercussions of this demand were to affect every aspect of Israelite culture as Samuel appreciated (I Sam 8:10-18). Culture is an integrated system, and the political changes occurring within the establishment were to have economic, social, and even religious effects.

The monarchy in many societies traces its ancestry back to legendary gods, and culture heroes. This led to many kings being considered as gods, becoming the focus of worship and supernatural sanctions. However, this could not be the case with Israel. The very humanness of the formation of the monarchy, and the failures of the first king, amplified the weakness of the whole institution.

A God-accepted Institution

The surprising paradox of this whole story is that although the monarchy was of human origin, God took it up and wove into it his redemptive purposes. The institution of the king was to become a new thread in God's revelation.

Although God allowed the Israelites to establish the same institution as the other nations it was to be wholly different in character. The laws in Deuteronomy 17:14-20 are unique to the ancient world. The king must first of all be a man whom God has chosen. Secondly, he must be an Israelite and not a foreigner. Thirdly, he should not accumulate wealth and possessions for himself. Finally, he must write a copy of the law for himself. These principles illustrate the fact that the king was required by God to enable Israel to fulfil the *shalom* lifestyle, and rule with righteousness and justice. Saul's failure to appreciate the nature of this role contrasted with the attitude of David.

Three major themes are initiated within this period which are to permeate the developing revelation of God. The first theme relates to that of King David himself. Although the humanness of David is clearly apparent within his biography, his desire for God is nevertheless strongly evident. The covenant that God makes with David (II Sam 7:10-16) has an eschatological dimension which the latter prophets were to apply to the coming Messiah. It was to be through the 'Son of David' that God's missionary purposes would be fulfilled.

Secondly, David desired to build a temple in which God could be worshipped, and in which he could dwell in a special way. As with the monarchy, the concept of the temple does not initiate with God, but it is taken up in God's redemptive purposes. Ezekiel takes up the imagery of the temple as the perfect restoration of God's purposes. In the New Testament, the Christians are called to 'know that your body is a temple of the Holy Spirit' (I Cor 6:19).

The third theme is that of the city of Jerusalem. David took over the existing centres of population to meet the administrative demands of the growing nation. Jerusalem, as the throne of God's appointed king, was to become the place to which all the nations would be drawn.

The *Shalom* Culture Today

The *shalom* culture was to be a witness to the nations by means of which they might see the glory of the Lord through his people. In this way other nations might be drawn to God, and enter into the blessing promised to Abraham.

Today, many writers have come to appreciate the value of the *shalom* of ancient Israel. However, we must avoid two errors in seeking to apply the concept to contemporary society. One is to regard this Old Testament lifestyle as merely part of God's spiritual revelation which has no remaining social relevance at all. We must realise that all the social and civil legislation and institutions of the Old Testament have significance in the principles they reveal. God is wanting his people in every generation to work out *shalom* in their own cultures, working for justice and freedom and ministering to the whole person.

The other error is to attempt a literal application of the strict provisions of the Law. These cannot be simply lifted out of the socio-economic context of ancient Israel and applied directly to the twentieth century. However, one must look at the principles behind the laws so as to interpret their principles today in one's own cultural context.

The *shalom* culture adds a big supplement to the cultural mandate. The Church of today would do well to discover a lifestyle which demonstrates the *shalom* of God in its own culture. In this way the nations might see the glory of the Lord in his Church. Even so, the mission of the Church must not be restricted to a matter of lifestyle. Israel's mission was to be a blessing to the nations, and an exclusive preoccupation with its own social life was to be a major danger facing the people of God.

Discussion Questions

1 Compare the *shalom* lifestyle of Israel before the monarchy with that characteristic of your own society.

2 How may the principles of Leviticus 25 be applied to our Western society? Think what they could mean for your own way of life.

3 Read Leviticus 19:33-34 and seek to put it into practice.

Recommended Reading

'An Evangelical Commitment to Simple Life-style', *Lausanne Occasional Paper* (No 20, 1980).

Ronald Sider, *Lifestyle in the Eighties* (Paternoster: Exeter, 1982).

Christopher Wright, *Living as the People of God* (IVP: Leicester, 1983).

Footnotes

1   T Wayne Dye, 'Toward a Cultural Definition of Sin', *Missiology* vol 4 (1976) No 1: pp 26-41.

2   Johannes Blauw, *The Missionary Nature of the Church* (Lutterworth Press: London, 1962) pp 21-27.

3   Alan Richardson, *A Theological Word Book of the Bible* (SCM Press: London, 1950) p 165.

4   Johannes Blauw, *op cit* p 24.

5   Ronald Sider, *Rich Christians in an Age of Hunger* (Hodder and Stoughton: London, 1977) p 79.

8

RELIGIOUS ENCOUNTER

In 1973, Bugongo was not even a preaching point in the Bu-
honga district. Today, this church has six baptised Christians,
130 probationers, and an average Sunday morning attendance
of 140. A large group was baptised at Christmas, 1978, from
Bugongo. The church received a plot of ground from the government at Bugongo so services could begin. A small church was
built of bamboo and grass. For several months only a few people
attended, most of them children.

It was very hard for the preacher to hold the attention of those
who came because 100 feet from the church was a site of pagan
worship. People brought their offerings of beans and beer to this
rock, called Nyamavuta, for the god of good fortune. Those
sitting inside the little church could watch the other worshippers
by the rock. Often, what was going on at the rock was more
interesting.

A vacation Bible school was planned for Bugongo. After a
day or two of classes, trying to hold the children's attention, the
preacher decided something had to be done. He and his helper
secured a sledge and bar to dig out Nyamavuta and smash him
to bits. The next day they announced their plans to those
attending Bible school. They just couldn't believe their ears,
because anyone attempting something like this would either go
crazy or die in a short time.

After the Bible school programme, the preacher and his helper
— in front of the small congregation — broke up the rock and dug
it out of the ground. Excitement ran high among the children.
They raced home to tell their parents what had happened. The
parents couldn't believe their ears. They said, 'The preacher will
go crazy or be dead by morning.'

In the morning the children, their parents, and others came to see what had happened to the preacher. They found him quite well and in his right mind. They said, 'Well, by tomorrow something will certainly happen.' They returned the next day and found that he was still well and sane. Their next reaction was, 'These men serve a god who is more powerful than ours.' Sick people began to come to the services; the preacher prayed for them and they recovered, many of them instantly. Those who were possessed with evil spirits came and were prayed for. They, too, were delivered and went home free . . . After a time, several witchdoctors, rain-makers, and other medicine men came to repent. They brought their wares to be burned. These items often cost thousands of francs, a sizeable investment in their economy.

The small church had to be enlarged; still not everyone could get in. Since then, a rock-walled, metal-roofed church has been built. It is already too small.[1]

Once the people of God were established in the Promised Land they were always subject to two temptations. The first was to isolate themselves from the surrounding nations in order to protect their own beliefs and practices, but in doing so they would fail to be the blessing to the nations that God intended. The second was for them to become so identified with the surrounding nations that nothing would distinguish them.

The Church of today faces the same dilemma. Does it withdraw from the issues of the world into its own closed society, or does it relate to the world? The first option may keep the purity of the faith, but it means that the message becomes irrelevant in a rapidly changing world. On the other hand, to identify may take away the very distinctiveness that makes the Church God's people with a prophetic message for mankind.

The Degeneration of the Kingship
With the establishment of the monarchy, Israel grew politically and militarily strong, and was able to take its place in the history of the nations. However, all too soon Israel

began to forget its covenant relationship and its mission. Military conquest and taxation can hardly be regarded as bringing blessing to the nations. The central, royal power began to degenerate into tyranny, and the people began to look back to the reign of David as a golden age.

The candid history of the monarchy in the Old Testament illustrates the constant moral challenge for those in high political office. Solomon achieved great advances for the nation, but only as a result of oppressive taxation and forced labour. Rehoboam, his successor, continued the policy and even tried to extend it, but the inevitable repercussion was rebellion and the division of the kingdom.

Jeroboam, who led the successful rebellion, typified the very character of much of the monarchy. His intense political ambitions led him to seek to harness religious traditions for his own purposes. In order to establish the newly created nation of the ten northern tribes, he manipulated the religion of Israel, and added to it other elements. He set up golden calves in the north and south of his kingdom, and said 'here are your gods, O Israel, who brought you up out of Egypt' (I Kings 12:28). New shrines were built on high places, and priests were appointed from any sort of people (I Kings 12:31-33). A syncretistic mixing of elements of traditional Canaanite religion was combined with that of the worship of Yahweh.

In the northern kingdom, the outward forms of religion all came under political control for the advantage of the state. Such a policy requires the silencing of all criticism that may challenge the system. However, this was a policy that was to lead to a clash of religions, and the judgement of Baal.

The Worship of Baal

Concept of Deity

The religious systems of the ancient world were fundamentally similar, being a complex form of polytheism based on the personification of natural forces. The purpose was to bring man and society into harmony with the rhythmic cycle of nature. This cycle of life and death was a delicately balanced system dependent upon the favour of the gods. The key notion was that of fertility. The seed of the sky (rain) fell upon the mother earth to bring forth the harvest of nature.

In many parts of the ancient Middle East, the male sky god was called *Baal*, meaning 'master', 'possessor', or 'husband'. The Baal cults affected and challenged the worship of Yahweh throughout the history of Israel. Perhaps the most dramatic story is that of the encounter with Elijah. In this case the Baal was Baal-melquart, the official deity of Tyre introduced into Hebrew society by Ahab's Tyrian wife Jezebel.

Baal was the storm god who brought rain, and one of his female consorts was Ashtaroth. The name was common in one form or another among many of the Semitic-speaking peoples of the area. The Israelites turned to the worship of Ashtaroth (or Astarte) soon after arriving in the land (Jdg 2:13, I Sa 7:3-4; 12:10). Ashtaroth was conceived of with a variety of aspects including that of fertility, love, and war — similar to Diana or Artemis among the Romans and Greeks.

Cultic Festivals

The festivals of Baal and Ashtaroth were essential to allow the people to co-operate with the gods in their fight against evil forces that would seek to bring chaos to the cycle of nature. Man had to stand on the side of the gods to perpetuate order and resist the fearful consequences of disorder. Three main festivals were common to Baal worship, although there was probably a multitude of local area festivals. The first major festival was a New Year's festival celebrating the victory of order over chaos in the continuing struggle, and this would result in a fruitful harvest later in the year. The second festival was at the beginning of spring, when the first rains came to bring life to the earth. The sexual symbolism here was strong, demonstrated in the temples with male and female prostitutes (Isa 57:5-9). The third consisted of the resurrection rites where the god of rains and vegetation was renewed in the autumn following his death in the heat of summer.

Fixed Social Structure

Within any such fertility cult the careful balance of nature leads to an immutable social and religious order. If any man dared resist the religious patterns, he risked the possibility of disturbing the whole cycle of nature with disastrous repercussions not only upon himself, but on the whole of his society. Although there are marked differences in the religious practices of the Canaanites from those of many tribal groups in the world today, it is remarkable how some of the same features can be identified.

Not only did this fear of disturbing the cycle of nature ensure the perpetuation of the religious cult, it also supported the existing social order. The name *Baal* meant master, and a slave would use the term of his human master. Baal was associated with the gods behind his master who supported the social hierarchy within society. Both masters and slaves held their positions because of the will of the gods. No one would think of striking out for social justice because it would only bring ill upon the whole community, rich and poor. J Bright notes, 'Ancient man knew nothing of social protest.'[2]

Power Encounter

The account of the confrontation of Elijah with the prophets of Baal provides a remarkable demonstration of the attitude of the prophets to Baalism within Israel. Some writers have focussed upon such events as a 'power encounter' between two religions.[3] The picture here is that of a conflict between two great deities to show which of them is the greatest and so 'entitled to' allegiance from the people of Israel.

Conflict of Lifestyles

Because it carries such fundamental ideas, any religion influences the whole culture of a people. As J H Bavinck has said, 'Culture is religion made visible.'[4] The encounter between Yahweh and Baal was not just a matter of two sets of religious ideas, but two whole cultures.

Yahweh	Baal
Man is a steward of the land	Land given to aristocracy
Lifestyle of moderation and concern for one's neighbour	Lifestyle of self-gratification
Concept of change and progress with a linear view of time	Status quo with a cyclic view of time

These two religious systems offered two radically conflicting lifestyles. God's intervention shows the gravity of the situation for the mission of Israel.

God's response was to send Elijah, who pronounced that there would be no dew or rain for the next two or three years (I Kings 17:1). This particular act is most significant as it touches the very centre of the cycle of nature. Yahweh challenges Baal where he is supposed to be most influential. The halting of the rains breaks the cycle of nature and therefore the whole structure of Baalism. The act also fulfils the promise given in Deuteronomy 11:16-17; 'Be careful or you will be enticed to turn away and worship other gods and bow down to them. Then the Lord's anger will burn against you, and he will shut the heavens so that it will not rain and the ground will yield no produce. . .'

The contest at Mount Carmel was most symbolic; however, for our purpose it is sufficient to consider the question: 'why fire from heaven?' By the time of Elijah, Baalism had developed more the concept of the sky god and associated Baal with the forces of fire and lightning. Once again Yahweh was challenging Baal where he was considered to be the most powerful, and once again Yahweh was shown to be God. This is the same pattern we noticed with the plagues, where Yahweh challenged the gods of Egypt.

An allied account is that of Naboth's vineyard, which further illustrated the principles of land ownership embedded in the religious consciousness of Israel (I Kings 21). Ahab was aware of the practice concerning land ownership in Israel, but Jezebel operated according to the customs of Baal. Failure to recognise and respect the rights of an individual and family within the covenant community led to judgement. Elijah emerged as the champion of the strong ethical demands of the Mosaic faith.

Gods and Idols

Many present-day writers consider the Old Testament concept of a conflict between gods to be an anathema. They would reject this traditional biblical interpretation because, with our modern understanding of a mechanistic universe, the notion of spirit powers in opposition to God are considered to be no more than the ideas of primitive peoples. Secondly, they would argue, in an event such as that at Mt Carmel one is witnessing only an unfortunate example of tribal religion. Today Western man is thought to have a more 'mature' view of religion, willing to accept the religious truth found in the faiths of other people. The answer to these arguments will be found by considering three primary aspects of Old Testament teaching.

Supernatural Powers

The Old Testament portrays the residence of Israel in the Promised land as a struggle between the syncretistic tendencies of Baalism and true Yahweh worship. The existence of supernatural forces in opposition to God was accepted as a reality, but the worship of such gods by Israel was condemned. Yahweh affirmed that he alone was to be their God and their allegiance was to be to him alone.

In the New Testament, Jesus was to speak of the 'power of the evil one', and Paul of the 'principalities and powers'. Many from Africa, Asia and Latin America have stressed to Western theologians the reality of evil powers and the necessity of demonstrating the supremecy of Jesus over them. For many people, conversion to Christ involves an encounter with power where people make a radical change of allegiance. People may have to destroy their idols, as with Gideon (Judges 6:25-32), or burn their books of magic (Acts 19:19). Such acts are crucial and significant steps in conversion.

Abou, for example, was a sorcerer living in Burkino Faso (in West Africa). He possessed the names of five evil spirits, each written in Arabic on special papers, and these gave him power to harm others. However, Abou had listened to a cassette tape giving the testimony of a Muslim who had experienced salvation in Christ. Abou was greatly moved, and he felt as though he was being chased by Jesus. Finally he gave in to Jesus, took those precious pieces of paper and buried them in a hole.

Soon afterwards Abou became sick with what Western doctors would call hepatitis, but this he regarded as a cleansing process. As soon as he was fully well Abou was eager to share his faith. Soon some sorcerers tried to curse him, but to no effect. They then used their magic powers to call up an evil spirit in the form of a snake to harm him, but again without success. There was no doubt whose power was greater, and Abou spent the time preaching Christ to the sorcerers.[5]

Westerners often find it difficult to conceive of the notion of supernatural forces, especially demonic forces in opposition to God. Perhaps this is an area in which we must be prepared to take a humble position and be willing to learn from Christians of different cultures. As we continue to develop the missionary themes of the Bible, this concept will be found to be increasingly relevant. Any biblical theology of mission must accept the demonic as a vital reality in any culture, and Christ must be demonstrated as Lord.

Foolishness of Idolatry

Within Baalism various symbols were used to portray the gods. This led to idolatry which was to plague Israelite society for centuries. Idolatry was condemned by the prophets as sheer foolishness. Nowhere is this more clearly seen than in the prophecies of Isaiah (Isa 44:9-20). Isaiah writes:

A tree is man's fuel for burning; some of it he takes and warms himself, he kindles a fire and bakes bread. But he also fashions a god and worships it . . . no-one has the knowledge or understanding to say, 'Half of it I used for fuel; I even baked bread over its coals, I roasted meat and I ate. Shall I make a detestable thing from what is left? Shall I bow down to a block of wood?' (Isa 44:15, 19).

Idols, images, and relics are common to most religions, including Christianity. Initially these items may be merely of assistance in worship, but they soon become the focus of worship itself. Although the prophets portray a strong monotheism and ridicule idolatry, they recognise that man cannot regard an idol as of no significance. The recognition and worship of idols infects the person with a spiritual blindness of heart and mind (Isa 44:18-20). Because of the reality of evil powers behind the idol, idolatry is a grave abomination to Yahweh, regarded as a spiritual adultery for Israel — and so is utterly condemned (Deut 7:25-26; 31:16; Hos 1:2).

Social Structure

One of the emphases of this chapter has been that a religion is not merely a set of religious ideas nor even a set of religious practices. All religions lie at the centre of a whole set of cultural ideas that affect the complete lifestyle of a people. In general, polytheism leads to a situation of status quo, as illustrated by Baalism. The coming of Christianity brings sweeping changes of ideas. When people accept Christianity they are accepting more than just a religion. The influence of that change will affect every part of their society.

Conversion from one religion to another can never be a mere intellectual exercise. Religion can never be separated from the rest of culture because as part of culture it forms an integrated whole. The Christian missionary can never say he has come to change the religion but not the culture; religious encounter will have repercussions throughout the entire way of life of a people. The missionary must therefore be fully aware of his responsibilities.

Discussion Questions
1 In the light of your understanding of Baal worship, describe the religion of a polytheistic people of which you have heard. How do their religious beliefs affect their social and economic life?
2 Read through the book of Acts and list the cases in which you can identify a 'power encounter'. How does the way the apostles deal with the demonic compare with the case of Elijah on Mount Carmel?
3 What would you say is the main aspect of your culture that would reveal a person's change of religious allegiance in becoming a Christian?

Recommended Reading
Allan Tippett, 'Conversion as a Dynamic Process in Christian Mission', *Missiology* (April 1977).
Allan Tippett, 'Verdict Theology in Missionary Theory' (*William Carey Library:* Pasadena, 1973).
Arthur Glasser, 'Power Encounter in Conversion from Islam', *The Gospel and Islam,* edited by Don McCurry (MARC: Monrovia, Ca, 1979): pp 129-139.

Footnotes
1   Donald Hohensee, *'Power Encounter* Paves Way For Church Growth in Africa', *Evangelical Missions Quarterly* (April 1979): pp 86-87.
2   John Bright, *The History of Israel* (SCM Press: London, 1974).
3   Alan Tippett, *Verdict Theology in Missionary Theory* (William Carey Library: Pasadena, 1973) pp 79-91.
4   J H Bavinck, *An Introduction to the Science of Mission* (Presbyterian & Reformed Pub Co: Philadelphia, 1960) pp 100-107.
5   Loren Entz, 'Challenge to Abou's Jesus', *Evangelical Missions Quarterly* Vol 22, No 1 (1986): pp 46-50.

9

THE CONSCIENCE
OF A NATION

I WAS HUNGRY:
you set going a humanistic association,
and you discussed my hunger.
Thank you.
I WAS NAKED:
and in your mind you debated
the morality of my appearance.
I WAS SICK:
and you knelt and thanked God
for your health.
I WAS HOMELESS:
you preached to me
of the spiritual shelter of the love of God.
I WAS LONELY:
and you left me alone
to pray for me.
You seem so holy,
so close to God.
But I am still hungry and lonesome,
and cold.
So where
have your prayers gone?
What does it profit a man
to page through his book of prayers
when the rest of the world
is crying for his help?[1]

The people of Israel were meant to demonstrate the character of their God to the nations of the world. One might therefore expect the message of the prophets to be directed towards the nations, whereas it was primarily directed to Israel itself and to the condemnation of her compromising attitude to other religions. The prophets were continually reminding Israel what it meant to be the people of God, calling the people back to the worship of the true God and to the *shalom* culture. Only through such a spiritual renewal might they enter into the blessing of God, and so become a society which reveals the life of God.

The prophets were concerned with the fact that Israel should fulfil her covenant promise. The mission of God was inseparably bound up with Israel and with Jerusalem, and no one could share in it without entering the covenant. This would entail becoming a proselyte, and so becoming part of Jewish society. 'The central concern of the prophets was to communicate to Israel what it meant to be Israel.'[2]

Condemnation of Israel

Like Gideon threshing the wheat, David tending his sheep and Elisha ploughing, Amos was at work in the fields when God first called him. He came from a town in Judah, and he preached to the people of the Northern Kingdom of Israel, about 760 BC. This was a time of great prosperity and apparent security for the nation. But Amos saw that prosperity was limited to the elite of society, and such wealth feeds on injustice.

His message forms the first of the prophets, which is recorded at length. Amos cries out at the many injustices within society, a message that is taken up by the prophets who follow him. Although the book of Amos commences with a denunciation of the surrounding nations – which would have been eagerly agreed to by the people of the Northern Kingdom – the message turns back onto them. With a penetrating perception Amos dissects the corruption of the Israelites and shows how far they have fallen from the lifestyle God intended.

Affluence Amidst Poverty

The wealth of the elite was gluttonous compared with the poverty which other Israelites endured. The wealthy enjoyed 'winter houses' and 'summer houses' (Amos 3:15), enjoyed luxurious living. '. . . You lie on beds inlaid with ivory and lounge on your couches. You dine on choice lamb and fattened calves. You strum away on your harps like David and improvise on musical instruments. You drink wine by the bowlful and use the finest lotions . . .' (Amos 6:4-6). All this occurred in the midst of poverty for the majority of the population.

Except in a completely regulated society there will always be different levels of income. Love for one's neighbour should lead to a just and generous sharing of the surplus, but this compassion was missing in Israel.

Oppression of the Poor

What was worse, the rich used their wealth and influence to oppress the poor to extract even greater luxuries for themselves.

> This is what the Lord says: 'For three sins of Israel, even for four, I will not turn back my wrath. They sell the righteous for silver, and the needy for a pair of sandals. They trample on the heads of the poor and upon the dust of the ground and deny justice to the oppressed.
>
> (Amos 2:6, 7)

Poverty is so often linked with injustice, and Amos very graphically describes God's anger towards those who oppress the poor (Amos 4:1, 5:11, 12; 8:4). Here one reads some of the harshest words in Scripture directed against the cultured, upper-class ladies of the day:

> Hear this word, you cows of Bashan on Mount Samaria, you women who oppress the poor and crush the needy and say to your husbands,

92

'Bring us some drinks!' The Sovereign Lord has sworn by his holiness: 'The time will surely come when you will be taken away with hooks, the last of you with fish-hooks.'

(Amos 4:1-2)

The individual members of a privileged class who profit from a corrupt social system and do nothing to change that structure stand guilty before God. Social evil is just as displeasing to God as personal sin. This is the truth that many liberation theologians have been trying to tell us. They have seen the importance of structural evil, while Western theologians have stressed the evil of personal sins. In fact both come under God's condemnation.

Structural evil is usually supported by an unjust legal system, and this was precisely the case with Israel. 'For I know how many are your offences and how great your sins. You oppress the righteous and take bribes and deprive the poor of justice in the courts' (Amos 5:12).

The rich used the law for their own benefit and greed. Corruption was rife with the use of false measures and tampered scales to cheat customers (Amos 8:5, 6). Bribery was commonplace. Amos, however, stresses the fact that God is concerned with the evils of an unjust society which exploits the weak and poor. These are not things which should be found amidst the people of God. 'Hate evil, love good; maintain justice in the courts' (Amos 5:15).

Hypocrisy in Worship
The basic thesis of the message of Amos is that true worship cannot exist where injustice is allowed to flourish; the division of social concern for other people from religious worship is nothing more than hypocrisy. This fact is taken over into the New Testament when John writes: 'If anyone says, "I love God", yet hates his brother, he is a liar. For anyone who does not love his brother, whom he has seen, cannot love God, who he has not seen' (I John 4:20).

93

But before John, Amos had written 'Away with the noise of your songs! I will not want to listen to the music of your harps. But let justice roll on like a river, righteousness like a never-failing stream' (Amos 5:23-24).

Even in the midst of their worship of Yahweh, the Hebrews continued to worship other gods. Sakkuth was the chief god, and Kaiwan was a god related to the morning star. These were Assyrian deities, and because Israel had made the Assyrian gods her own she would, in turn, be taken captive by the Assyrians.

The Day of the Lord

The high point of Jewish history was as we saw the reign of King David. Israel was established not only as a nation in its own right, but as a nation with considerable influence upon other nations. After David and Solomon, the nation was divided into North and South, and the gradual decline began. The people began to look back to the rule of David as the golden days of Israel, and forward to a new day when God would restore his people.

They expected that this new kingdom would be a military and political empire like that of David. These nationalistic tendencies were to spring forth on many occasions in the history of Israel; for many the kingdom of God would be a Jewish empire, with little spirituality about it.

The Day of Judgement

The popular notion of the 'Day of the Lord' was that Yahweh would intervene in history and establish Israel as the head of all the nations. This act would not depend on the faithfulness of Israel. However, the shocking message of Amos and the other prophets was that judgement would begin with Israel. Just because Israel is the elect of God would not mean that it would avoid judgement. Because the people know him, they are more at fault when they disobey his Law.

The Day of the Lord is thus the occasion when Yahweh would actively intervene in history to punish sin. When the

Israelites were an oppressed people in Egypt, they had seen God's passion for justice. But that passion is like a two-edged sword, for when they became the oppressors, it led to their destruction.

It is all too easy to concentrate upon individual sins and neglect the issues of corruption within a society. In the last few years writers such as Ronald Sider[3] have been correcting the balance and showing the reality of God's concern with evil social structures. There is an important difference between consciously willed individual acts of sin and the passive participation in evil social structures. However, the Bible shows that God is concerned about both.

Yahweh – Lord of the Nations

Although the major part of the book of Amos is directed towards Israel, God's concern is shown to be wider than just that of his people. The oracles of chapters 1 and 2 of Amos show the future judgement by God of the nations. Yahweh is revealed as Lord of the surrounding nations and not just Israel. "'Are not you Israelites the same to me as the Cushites?" declares the Lord. "Did I not bring Israel up from Egypt, the Philistines from Caphtor and the Arameans from Kir?"' (Amos 9:7).

One remarkable aspect of God's authority over the nations is seen in his use of them to fulfil his purposes for Israel. The most notable example is that of King Cyrus, described by Isaiah as the Lord's 'anointed'. 'This is what the Lord says to his anointed, to Cyrus, whose right hand I take hold of to subdue nations before him and to strip kings of their armour, to open doors before him so that gates will not be shut' (Isa 45:1).

The God of the Israelites may have been regarded as a national deity by the ordinary people, but this was certainly not the case with the prophets. They saw Yahweh as the only God, the Lord of all nations. He sets up Gentile rulers and also pulls them down. The authority of any king derives from the paramount authority of the Lord himself. His concern must therefore be universal.

Frequently, missionaries speak in a parochial way about

'closed countries', but it is essential to recognise that God is sovereign over all nations. Many were horrified when the missionaries were put out of China by the communists in 1948 and thought that the time of church growth in that land had come to an end. Yet in 1985 it was estimated that there were some 20 times as many Christians in that land as when the missionaries had left.[4] Clearly, God is preparing people through history in their responsiveness to his revelation. On a human level one may speak of people becoming more responsive as a result of migration or military conquest,[5] but one must recognise that at a higher level God is sovereign.

Exile

In 722 BC, the Assyrian armies threatened the kingdoms of Israel and Judah. Samaria fell and the peoples of the Northern Kingdom were taken into captivity. According to Assyrian chronicles, over 27,000 people were deported by Sargon II, the effect being to terminate the Northern Kingdom as an independent, homogeneous state.

In 587 BC, Jerusalem stood at the brink of a similar catastrophe. Judah's fate was inevitable. The Babylonian forces took Jerusalem, burnt down the temple and the royal palace, which ended the independent reign of David's line. Large numbers of the surviving citizens were deported to Babylonia. There they were relatively free to establish themselves as part of the community, to maintain their own traditions and even practise their own religion if they wanted to. Still, the physical suffering of the people of Israel was almost indescribable. The book of Lamentations expresses something of the writer's grief over the suffering and humiliation of his people. But, at a deeper level, the writer laments the fact that God had rejected His people because of their sin.

The warning of the prophets had not been heeded, and God had executed his judgement. In time, Babylon itself would be judged for her actions (Isa 47), but the blessing promised to Abraham was not to fail. Even in the midst of the warning of judgement, the prophets held out a promise of a future restoration — a new hope. The Lord says: 'In that day I will restore David's fallen tent. I will repair its broken places, restore its ruins, and build it as it used to be' (Amos 9:11).

Discussion Questions
1 If we compare the average lifestyle of a European or North American with that of a typical person from Africa, Asia, or Latin America, Western lifestyle is far more luxurious than that found in Israel at the time of Amos. What should be our response to meeting the needs of the world's poor at this current time?

2 Evaluate and consider Christian motives and methods in giving aid to people in need.

3 What do you consider should be the Christian attitude to unjust economic structures? What should be his response to the situation?

Recommended Reading
Ronald J Sider, *Rich Christians in an Age of Hunger* (Hodder & Stoughton: London, 1978).

John V Taylor, *Enough is Enough* (SCM Press: London, 1975).

John White, *The Golden Cow* (Marshalls: Basingstoke, 1979).

J A Motyer, *The Day of the Lion* (IVP: Leicester, 1974).

Footnotes
1 Anonymous, adapted from *Handbook on World Development* (Shaftesbury Project: Nottingham, 1983) p 144.

2 W Brieggemann, *Tradition for Crises* (John Knox Press: Edinburgh, 1968) p 25.

3 Ronald J Sider, *Rich Christians in an Age of Hunger* (Hodder & Stoughton: London, 1977).

4 Silas Hong, *The Dragon Net* (Victory Press: Eastbourne, 1976).

5 Donald McGavran, *Understanding Church Growth* (Eerdmans: Grand Rapids, 1970) pp 218-227.

10

SUFFERING – A DILEMMA IN MISSION

The Temple's gone!

Who can describe the sight? Who can put down in words the stopping of the heart, the disbelief of the eyes, the feeling that the world had changed. As surely as the mind knew that our Temple had been the work of men, so did the soul know that God had guided those men, that God had had a hand in it, that God had lived there. In the Holy of Holies, unseen but there. Who could doubt it? Our mothers had told us so, our fathers, our teachers.

Now the Temple was a wasteland of rubble, wherein old men sat and wept into their beards. Where did God live now? Who could tell, in the vast field of ruin, even where the Holy of Holies had been? Where the great Altar, where the towering pillars of the Sanctuary, where the beautiful Gates of Nicanor, where the lovely Courts and Chambers had been? Did God himself now sit in the dusty stones, weeping?

I looked around. The colonnades which had edged the Temple Area, which had looked as if they would last for centuries, had great gaps, and in their remains people were living, in holes, like animals.[1]

It has already been noted that suffering entered human experience with the Fall (chapter 3). Not only must the people of God recognise that mission will be carried out within a suffering world, but also appreciate that mission itself will involve suffering.

The Arena of Suffering

Whether it is the crushing pain of starvation, or the maiming caused by a shell in war, or the engulfing waters of a tidal wave, man has experienced suffering. The immense suffering that the people of Israel faced during the seige and fall of Jerusalem only illustrates the enigma of suffering.

Even writing about the subject leaves one with a sense of awe. What experience does the writer have of some of the fearful suffering lived through by some of our race? Who can analyse such a topic without knowing tears, and realising that he is failing to appreciate some of the deepest feelings that humankind can know? It is so often amidst suffering that people cry out, 'Why, God?' What answers do they receive through the tears?

Since mission takes place in the midst of human suffering, it must therefore not be ignored but understood as the arena in which Christian love and compassion can be manifest. Man is continually confronted by many and varied needs: Emotional suffering is perhaps less dramatic than physical pain, but it is more common and perhaps more difficult to bear. A broken heart can be more hurtful than an aching tooth.

Disasters consist of massive suffering amongst whole societies. In such situations it is not possible to speak of the total suffering as, somehow, the suffering of one individual multiplied by the number of individuals involved. The suffering experienced by others in one's family only heighten one's own pain. What is the cause of such agony? How can it be that some human beings have to face such shattering experiences?

Some have tried to draw a distinction between natural ('acts of God') and unnatural (man-made) disasters. Although the differentiation may seem inadequate, it does reveal the general thinking we have about the source of suffering. First, there is that which has its origin from human action, and secondly, there is that which is outside human control. It is a sad fact of geography that certain areas of the globe are more prone to natural hazards such as cyclones and earthquakes. Whether the disaster is natural or unnatural, however, it is the poorest members of a community who tend to suffer most from the effects.

Human Wickedness

Much of human suffering is caused by the effects of one person upon another. Jesus said, 'For from within, out of men's hearts, come evil thoughts, sexual immorality, theft, murder, adultery, greed, malice, deceit, lewdness, envy, slander, arrogance and folly' (Mk 7:21). James writes, 'You want something but don't get it. You kill and covet, but you cannot have what you want' (James 4:2). The immense amount of human suffering caused by human actions need not be stressed — it is all too obvious. Fifteen million people were killed in World War I, and 34 million in the Second World War. Murders, rapes, riots, and crimes are continually part of our news.

The biblical answer to the question, 'Why do men do such things?' is found in the teaching on the Fall. Here evil entered the world and was embraced by humankind. Humanists have sought to argue that society is gradually improving as man is evolving in his development. The history of the twentieth century has shattered such an evolutionary view, and has illustrated too clearly the sinful nature of man.

Suffering is not just caused by the direct wilfulness of man. It may also be caused by unjust social systems in which the greed of the rich deprive the poor of the little they have. It may be caused by over-intensive farming, loss of topsoil and desertification, producing all the conditions for a famine long before the drought brings the catastrophe. The tragic famines that have wracked the people of Africa in the 1980's have 'not been brought about by meteorological catastrophe, but by man-made mistakes of policy and planetary management.'[2]

Looking at the causes of human suffering in these terms one is willing to agree with C S Lewis when he writes, 'When souls become wicked they will certainly use this possibility to hurt one another; and this, perhaps, accounts for four-fifths of the sufferings of men . . . . Even if all suffering were man-made, we should like to know the reason for the enormous permission to torture their fellows which God gives to the worst of men.'[3]

God and Human Suffering

When tragedy strikes an individual so often the question that is asked is 'Why does this have to happen to me?' Even the most convinced atheist finds it difficult to consider his own misfortune as the one chance in a million. Statistical averages may be acceptable when dealing with the suffering of others, but not with one's own. Here a deeper answer is required to the question.

The book of Job was probably one of the first books of the Bible to deal with this very question. Space does not allow a full exploration of the various ideas in the book, but it is sufficient to consider the central ideas expounded by each of the characters in the story.

Eliphaz is the first of the friends to speak to the suffering Job. The key element in his advice is acceptance. In each of his three speeches he counsels Job to accept something — the discipline of God, the punishment of God, and the fact that Job must be at fault. Job cannot accept this view because he knows not everyone is suffering as he is. Although partly true, such advice is unhelpful and upset rather than comforted Job.

Bildad's speeches are short and concise. His major point is that all men are sinners. None, including Job, is righteous. His view of God is a lofty one, but it contains no element of mercy. God relates to mankind as judge, and Job is now being punished for his sins. This applies to all men, but Bildad gives no explanation of why some notable sinners prosper all their lives, while apparently righteous men suffer.

Zephar's idea is that God's laws are fixed and he rewards and punishes evil. He argues through the following sequence: God's laws are fixed; good men prosper; evil men are punished; if Job suffers it is because he has done evil. As with Bildad's argument, the formula does not match the facts of life.

Elihu is the last of the friends to speak, and he is the youngest. He provides yet another dimension to the discussion in proposing that God reveals himself in many different ways to different people. God primarily reveals himself through laws that bring justice, and through nature which he controls. Elihu asks Job to recognise the greatness and power of God, but he does not explain why an all-powerful God does not turn injustice into justice, poverty into prosperity, and pain into joy. These are the questions that Job needed to have answered, and unless our faith can provide answers to these questions in our own situation, it is of little value. Job was concerned about justice now, not just in the life to come.

Finally, into the situation comes the revelation of God. Job wanted to know the charge against him, and the reason for his suffering. God does not tell him, but he does assert (Job chapters 38-40) that, as Creator and sustainer of the universe, his power is supreme over all things. The most important thing to understand in the midst of suffering is that God knows our plight and is all powerful. What he allows is ultimately for our good. When God restores Job's fortunes, this demonstrates not only God's power, but also His justice and His love. God blesses not just with material things, but with intangible things such as love, joy and peace.

The Evil One

In chapter 3 it was noted that evil did not originate within the human world, but from the supernatural realm. This is yet another aspect to the complex issue of suffering — the existence of the Evil One. The whole dialogue of Job is set within this context. Beyond the personal experience of Job is another dimension in which Satan appears before God and asks to test Job (Job chapters 1-2). Two points can be deduced from the story. First, the evil intruder is a person, and secondly, that person is limited in his influence by the constraints of God himself.

Several times in the New Testament Satan is specifically related to sickness. Luke 13 tells the story of a woman who had an evil spirit that made her ill for 18 years: she was bent over and could not straighten up. Mark 5 tells of the demonised man: 'Night and day among the tombs and in the hills he would cry out and cut himself with stones' (Mark 5:5).

Satan is portrayed in Scripture as one who has come to spoil and destroy the work of God. Evil is not a force or influence which pervades the universe, but a person. In the New Testament it is clear that Jesus speaks of Satan as a person, and not just as a personification of evil. When Jesus is confronted by people bound by Satan he is moved with compassion. He wants to see those in bondage released into the fullness of life that God intended for that person.

A telling illustration of the work of Satan is seen in the parable of the weeds in Matthew 13:24-30, 36-45. This is one of the few parables to which Jesus gives an explanation. The good seed is sowed by the king, whilst an enemy comes and sows weeds. In order to avoid harming the good crop, the king forbids his workers to pull up the weeds because in so-doing they harm the good harvest. The world is a mixture of good and evil, and since God is concerned to obtain a good harvest, the weeds are tolerated for the time being.

In any discussion on suffering it is too easy to focus excessively upon the role of Satan in causing pain, or to focus only on the human aspect. The truth is far more complex, and the various elements combine in a multitude of ways.

Attitude of God

Suffering is a subject to which all the major religions of the world address themselves in one way or another. Islam conceives of Allah as being transcendent and utterly detached from creation. Since mankind is like the pieces on a chess-board and Allah is the only player, human beings must therefore accept their fate with patience. The only word of comfort offered to a suffering world is the cry, 'It is the will of Allah'.

Buddhism, on the other hand, seeks a radically different solution expressed in the 'four noble truths'. First, life means to suffer. Secondly, this suffering is caused by men's

103

desires. Thirdly, to escape from suffering, man must rid himself of desires and cravings. Finally, to be freed from desires one must follow the path of the Buddha until ultimately one attains the extinction of desires — Nirvana. The Bible presents a totally different view of suffering from either of these religions. It describes three important principles showing the attitude of God to human sufferings.

God never enjoys judging people God longed for his people to repent. He continually offered Israel the opportunity of reversing the flow of history even as the Babylonian armies advanced. If they would only repent and turn from their wicked ways he would forgive them (Jer 7:5-7). God is by his very nature just and judged his people according to their deeds (Jer 17:10). The judgement matched the sin; the oppressors became the oppressed (Jer 12:7f). Never let it be said, however, that God enjoys punishing people.

God enters into human suffering God does not stand outside human suffering but enters into human pain. This most remarkable aspect of the biblical revelation was to realise itself in all its fullness in the Incarnation and later in the Cross.

Father Damien, a priest, worked for many years among the lepers of Molokai, a small island in the Pacific Ocean. Each Sunday he would conduct worship services, and often he would begin with the words, 'You who are lepers': the people listened politely to what he had to say. Then, one day he began his sermon with the words, 'We who are lepers': they looked at the white patches on his skin, and they knew that he understood, and they listened.[4]

God is the source of hope A key element in any disaster is the need for hope. Many people are imprisoned not by iron bars, but by hopelessness. When people have no hope, they have nothing to live for, and nothing to work for. Restoration must start through the kindling of a spark of hope which can burst forth into the fire of a new life. In the midst of the desolation of a destroyed Jerusalem Jeremiah cries,

Because of the Lord's great love we are not consumed, for his compassions never fail. They are new every morning; great is your faithfulness. I say to myself, 'The Lord is my portion; therefore I will wait for him.'

(Lam 3:22-24)

Discussion Questions

1 Read the book of Lamentations and see how it opens various insights relating to refugees in the world today.

2 Consider the attitude of Buddha, Mohammed, and Jesus to the subject of suffering. How do the various concepts of God found in these three religions influence the behaviour of the followers to human suffering? You may want to read *A Book of Beliefs* (Lion Publishing: Tring, 1981).

3 How would you seek to counsel an enquirer interested in becoming a Christian when you know that to make such a decision will result in fanatical opposition from his family and society?

Recommended Reading

John W Wenham, *The Enigma of Evil* (IVP: Leicester, 1985).

C S Lewis, *The Problem of Pain* (Fontana Books: London, 1940).

Footnotes

1   David Kossoff, *The Voices of Masada* (Mitchell Valentine: London, 1973), pp 110-112, seeking to describe the feelings of a handful of survivors from the Dead Sea fortress of Masada on their return to Jerusalem after it had been destroyed by the Romans in 70 AD.

2   *Famine: A man-made disaster? A Report for the Independent Commission on International Humanitarian Issues.* (Pan Books: London, 1985), back cover.

3   C S Lewis, *The Problem of Pain* (Fontana Books: London 1940) p 77.

4   Geoffrey Hanks, *Island of No Return – the Story of Father Daimen of Molokai* (The Religious Education Press: Oxford, 1978).

11

THE MISSION OF THE TRUE ISRAEL

Walk With Us

Be patient with us as a people
Don't judge us backward simply because we don't follow your
stride.

Be patient with our pace
Don't judge us lazy simply because we can't follow your tempo.

Be patient with our symbols
Don't judge us ignorant because we can't read your signs.

Be patient with us and proclaim the richness of your life which
you share with us.

Be with us and be open to what we can give
Be with us as a companion who walks with us,
Neither behind nor in front
In our search for life and ultimately for God.

Help us to discover our own riches
Don't judge us poor because we lack what you have.

Help us discover our chains
Don't judge us slaves by the types of shackles you wear.[1]

Amidst the emotional shock of a people taken into captivity,
beaten, and made slaves, with no temple and no Jerusalem,

God spoke through his prophets. Through the darkness of the conquest God revealed the outline of a new beginning. There would be a New Covenant between a forgiving God and his repentant people. There would be a new exodus back to the Promised Land, with a new opportunity for Israel to accomplish her mission.

The Remnant

God promised to shake the people of Israel like sieved corn (Amos 9:9). However, God also promised to retain a 'remnant' through whom he would continue to fulfil his purposes — the true Israel.

The True Israel

Amos is the first to use the term remnant, and he does so with a sense of bitter irony: the remnant remaining of Israel will be a bit of a leg saved from the wolves (3:12), or a smouldering stick rescued from the fire (4:11). Isaiah developed the concept of the 'remnant'. The nation of Israel must be punished for her sins, but like a tree that had been cut down, sap remained and a 'shoot' would one day emerge (Isa 6:13; 11:1). Isaiah even named one of his sons 'Shear-jashub', a remnant shall return (7:3). Through the fiery trial there will emerge a purified remnant, truly trusting in the Lord (Isa 10:20-23). These are the True Israel who would be a witness to the nations.

Nominality

Within every major religion one finds the problem of nominalism. This was Israel's problem, and it is also the problem that faces the Christian Church in many parts of the world. The *World Christian Encyclopaedia*[2] states that professing Christians in the UK are 86.9% of the population, while a recent survey[3] has shown that only 11% of adults attend church. Similar results are found in other parts of the world where the Church has not had such a long history. In Ghana 52% of the population call themselves Christian, but only about 5% actually attend church.[4]

The reasons for nominalism are many: intellectual problems, disenchantment with the established Church as an institution, pleasure-seeking lifestyle, and personal problems which alienate people from the Church.[5] Some of these issues can be seen within the life of Israel. First, for example, the priests who had been called to a special task of service to God often used their position for their own gain. The sons of Eli abused their role, and exploited the people (I Sam 2:12-17). Secondly, the continual cry of Israel was that the people wanted to be like the other nations, though God wanted them to be distinct. The people wanted a king as had other countries (I Sam 8:5), while God wanted them to recognise him as their king. Thirdly, the people continually showed a greater concern with material possession than with their God. In these examples we observe that the fundamental factor behind nominalism is frequently a preoccupation with the creation rather than the Creator. From the Fall man has looked to the material world to obtain his needs and find fulfilment. On the other hand, God has wanted a people who would put him first and find their meaning and hope in him.

The Spiritual Israel

Isaiah distinguishes the political Israel from the spiritual. God rules over the remnant, and in them he will triumph in history. The remnant is a 'narrowing down' of the people of God — who will be the vehicle of God's redemptive purposes, bringing the blessing promised to the nations.

Israel was utterly humbled, but God promises to give them a 'new heart and a new mind' (Ezek 36:26), and to put his spirit within them (Ezek 36:27). Ezekiel adds the image of a vast valley with the dried bones of a discarded nation and predicts a renewal of life and activity (37:1-14).

The Messiah

The theme of the remnant is closely linked with that of the Messiah. God's realistic view of the remnant recognises that they were not always righteous. Sometimes the prophets speak as though God has only spared the remnant as a link to a yet brighter future (Amos 3:12; 4:11; Isa 1:9), a future which would be ushered in by the coming of the Messiah. There are three major Messianic models in the Old Testament.

Son of David

The inadequacies of the dynasty of David actually encouraged the notion of the Messiah. The people looked back to the rule of David as the golden age of Israel's history. However, the prophets encouraged the people to look forward to the coming of the Son of David, God's appointed king, who would rule in righteousness (Isa 9:1-7; Micah 4:1-4). Once again the universal scope of the prophets is seen in the gathering of the nations: 'In that day the Root of Jesse will stand as a banner for the peoples; the nations will rally to him, and his place of rest will be glorious' (Isa 11:10).

Son of Man

Another outstanding model is that of the Son of Man, found most commonly in the apocalyptic literature – for example Daniel 7:13, 14. Here the Son of Man is seen as an apocalyptic character set outside of history, but breaking into it to establish his rule. His kingdom will not be limited to Israel, but will extend over all the nations of the earth. 'He was given authority, glory and sovereign power; all peoples, nations and men of every language worshipped him. His dominion is an everlasting dominion that will not pass away, and his kingdom is one that will never be destroyed' (Dan 7:14). Jesus on many occasions referred to himself as the Son of Man (Mark 8:38; 13:26; 14:62). He obviously used the term in the context of Daniel 7:13f, but he added to the meaning something which both enriched it and gave it new meaning: 'For even the Son of Man did not come to be served, but to serve, and to give his life as a ransom for many' (Mark 10:45).

The Suffering Servant

A third model is the greatest in that it gives a view into the very heart of God's plan to accomplish his mission; we find this in the four great Servant passages:

First Song: Isa 42:1-7
Second Song: Isa 49:1-6
Third Song: Isa 50:4-9
Fourth Song: Isa 52:13 — 53:12

It must be realised that 'servant' is not used in a derogatory sense in the Old Testament. The Hebrew word used is *ebed*, which carries the meaning of one who has surrendered certain rights in return for others. The *ebed* would serve his master, whom he would regard as a 'father' to him, one who would care for him and guide him. This is a different concept from the Greek word *doulos* which is also translated in the English Bible by the word 'slave'. In Greek culture, the *doulos* (slave) was no more than an object for work. The term *ebed* in religious usage carried the meaning of an individual accepting a humble position before God. It stresses God's total claim upon the person's life, and an obedience to do God's will. The greatest characteristic of the servant of God is a desire to do the will of God. As Hudson Taylor wrote, 'The greatest mission is submission.'

There has been much debate as to the nature of the servant of the Lord. Some have argued that it was Israel, and others that it was the Christ — the personification of Israel become the person himself. The analysis provided by the German scholar Franz Delitzche has proved to be most useful. He writes:

> The idea of 'the servant of Jehovah' assumes, to speak figuratively, the form of a pyramid. The base was Israel as a whole; the central section was that of Israel, which was not merely Israel according to the flesh, but according to the spirit also; the apex is the person of the Mediator of salvation springing out of Israel. And the last of the three is regarded (1) as the centre of the circle of the promised kingdom — the second David; (2) the centre of the circle of the people of salvation — the second Israel; (3) the centre of the circle of the human race — the second Adam.[6]

110

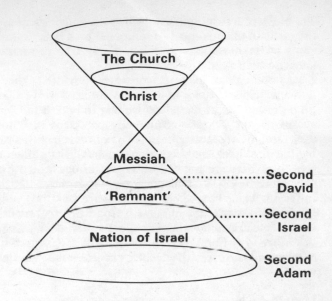

Fig 11:1

Delitzche's Model: The Servant of Jehovah

Figure 11:1 illustrates Delitzche's analysis; it shows that this model focussed the centre of the missionary purposes of God upon his servant. He is the one who will carry the light of true religion to all people. However, the means by which God will accomplish this task is most disturbing: He will not use force to establish his kingdom, but through suffering and death he will bring salvation to many. This was an aspect of God's mission that Israel could not comprehend, one that the Church today can easily fail to grasp. The sufferings of the servant were not only the consequence of his mission, but the very condition of its success.

The Suffering Church

The future Church, 'the second Israel' in continuing the missionary task of the servant, must recognise that suffering is not only a possibility, but is indispensable for its mission.

The element of triumphalism which has sometimes entered the ranks of mission must be tempered by a deep humility, and a willingness to serve others. Those who proclaim the Cross must also carry the Cross! (John 12:23)

Paul recognised this principle when he wrote to the Corinthians, 'Now I rejoice in what was suffered for you, and I fill up in my flesh what is still lacking in regard to Christ's afflictions, for the sake of his body, which is the church' (Col 1:24). Many explanations have been given of this verse, but the most likely interpretation is that 'Christ's afflictions' spoken of here are not the actual sufferings which Christ experienced by way of his vicarious atonement, but those sufferings which he foretold for the Church.

The fulfilment of the mission of God will entail hardship, as well illustrated by the Apostle Paul when he lists his sufferings in II Cor 11:24-26. Like Paul, the Church in its mission will enter into the deepest experiences of a suffering world.

Light to the Nations
The central nature of the mission of Israel to the nations is expressed vividly in Isaiah 2:2-4, and in Micah 4:1-3. These passages illustrate the centrality of the mountain of the Lord and show the people of the earth making a pilgrimage towards that mountain. The passages bear close examination, as explained below, because there are many recurring themes within the picture:

1 The exaltation of the mountain or the temple (Mic 4:1; Isa 60:1).

2 The pilgrimage of the nations to the mountain of God (Mic 4:1; Isa 6:3; Isa 66:19-21). 'Come, let us go up to the mountain of the Lord, to the house of the God of Jacob' (Mic 4:2).

3 '. . . to you the riches of the nations will come' (Isa 60:5). Psalm 87 is a hymn in praise of Jerusalem in which the nations traditionally hostile to Israel will be called to be among its people.

4 On the mountain the nations will be instructed.

5 God will establish the *shalom* lifestyle. War will be ended,

as will the exploitation of the poor and weak (Mic 4:3-4).
6 There the people will worship the Lord. This is the supreme goal of the pilgrimage. '. . . for my house will be called a house of prayer for all nations' (Isa 56:7; Isa 66:23; Ps 22:27-29).

The great prophecies had foretold that the salvation of God would reach all humankind through Israel. Yet few pondered the implications of such an honour, much less sought to put it into action. Following Israel's return from exile under Ezra and Nehemiah, Israel became progressively exclusive. In an attempt to preserve their faith and religious practice, Israel withdrew from social contact with the other nations and looked with contempt upon 'the Gentile dogs'.

The tension that arises from being 'in the world, but not of it' is one with which the Church has had to struggle throughout its history. To emphasise the aspect of being 'in the world' can lead to compromise and a loss of the distinctiveness of the Church. On the other hand, to stress the aspect of being 'not of the world' can lead to isolation and a lack of relevance — never mind a lack of love.

Jonah – a Challenge to Israel

The book of Jonah is unique in many ways among the Old Testament writings. We do not know who wrote the book, nor even what happened to Jonah himself. However, the message is clear. God wanted to rebuke Israel's distorted understanding of her status before him. He wanted to rebuke her nationalistic, self-righteous pride.

Jonah is not portrayed as a missionary. He does not call the people of Nineveh to leave their gods and worship Yahweh, nor even call them to repentance. He merely exposes their sins and proclaims a coming judgement. The key to understanding the story is seen in Yahweh seeking to reveal to his stubborn prophet his compassion for even the cruel city of Nineveh. God does not delight in the judgement of any people but prefers to forgive their sins; the people must, however, first repent.

The book of Jonah is not a book issuing a mandate for

113

aggressive missionary outreach but a revelation of God's love for all nations. Only later – when the Messiah lives through the Jonah experience in his own death, burial, and resurrection – does there develop a broader concept of mission within this book. One lesson that applied to Jonah, Israel, and the Church today concerns our attitude to those outside the people of God. Jonah's lack of love contrasted with the great compassion of God even to a sinful people. Love must be the driving force within the mission of the people of God.

Discussion Questions

1 If you were to give a message on JONAH THE SERVANT OF GOD, which of his good points and bad points would you mention?
2 Consider the place of suffering in the missionary task (Refer to Eph 3:1, 13; II Tim 2:8ff; II Cor 4:10f).
3 What are some of the factors which produce nominal Christians in your country? In what ways may the Church itself be the cause of nominalism?

Recommended Reading

Johannes Blauw, *The Missionary Nature of the Church* (Lutterworth Press: London, 1974).
H H Rowley, *Israel's Mission to the World* (Student Christian Movement Press: London, 1939).
F F Bruce, *Israel and the Nations* (Paternoster Press: Exeter, 1963).
Peter Brierley, 'Church Nominalism – the Plague of the Twentieth Century', *MARC Monograph No 2* (MARC Europe: London, 1985).
Peter Brierley, 'Introduction', *UK Christian Handbook 1987/88* (MARC Europe: London, 1986).

Footnotes

1 Anonymous
2 David Barrett, *World Christian Encylopaedia* (Oxford University Press: Oxford, 1982) p 699.

3 Peter Brierley, *Prospects for the Eighties, Vol 2* (MARC Europe: London, 1983) pp 6-7.

4 *Brong Ahafo Regional Congress on Evangelism* (New Life For All: Accra, 1985).

5 *Lausanne Occasional Paper No 23 — Christian Witness to Nominal Christians among Protestants* (LCWE: Illinois, 1980) pp 5-7.

6 C F Keil & F Delitzshe, *Commentary on the Old Testament, Vol VII, part 2* (Eerdmans: Grand Rapids, 1970) p 174.

12

THE PERIOD BETWEEN THE TESTAMENTS

A missionary in India was invited by a small group of low-caste people to share with them the message of the Christian faith. They were very poor people who lived in simple mud huts. On the appointed day the missionary gathered with about 12 adults in one of their homes. A water buffalo and some chickens were in one corner of the room; there was little or no ventilation, and only a small oil lamp which provided faint light. The floor of the hut was dried cow dung. The missionary sat on a mat on the floor with the group and patiently shared with them the story of Christ and the meaning of the Gospel. After several visits and much prayer, the little group trusted in Christ as their Saviour and received Christian baptism. A church was born!

Some time later, on one occasion when the missionary was visiting these new converts, one of the men said to him, 'Missionary, do you know why we listened so attentively to your words when you first came to us? It was not just what you told us that caught our attention, though the story of Christ was very wonderful and touched our hearts. It was the fact that you as a rich American (rich in their eyes) were willing to come into our humble homes, sit on the dirt floor, eat our meager food, and make yourself at home with us, that really convinced us that what you were saying was true and caused us to listen with a whole heart.[1]

The 400-year period between the Testaments reveals a major change in the people of Israel. There is a great difference between what one sees in the Old Testament and the Judaism found in the Gospels. Before beginning to look at the New Testament it is helpful to follow some of the major issues of change. These have a great influence on the concept of mission that will come into its full flower in the New Testament.

The Diaspora (The Dispersal)

The ancient world was characterised by continual movements of peoples, and the Jews were no exception. The early dispersions of the Jews were largely voluntary, undertaken for a variety of reasons, among which trade was important. Notably, though the Jews were distant from their ancient lands, they never lost their sense of identity.

The Jewish contacts with Arabia, for example, go back further than the time of the Queen of Sheba. A major shipping trade route existed along the coast of Arabia, and documents tell of fleets of trading ships leaving for India and the East. The story is told that when Ezra wrote to call the Jews to return to Jerusalem, the Jews in Yemen refused because they had come to love the land so much. Ezra is said to have become angry with them and cursed them. The curse was supposed to say that they would experience great misery and never know lasting happiness.[2]

The Jews also had close connections with Persia. Large numbers of Jews remained in Babylon after the migration back to Jerusalem under Ezra. Neither the Babylonians nor the Persians interfered with the inner religious and social life of the Jews. They were allowed to live on a level of equality with the majority of the people, and some achieved prominence in the court.

Early trade contacts are also known to have occurred with India.[3] However, it was after the destruction of the second temple by Titus (70 AD) that some 100,000 Jews are reported to have migrated to India. St Thomas was supposed to have met Jews in South India during the first century.

Another Eastern country, China, was known to the Jews during the days of Isaiah by the name *Sinim* (see Isa 49:12).

However, the earliest date of known migration was not until about 100 BC.

That the Jews had a strange longing for Egypt can be seen throughout the Old Testament. Trade routes to Egypt were followed by Jews throughout their history. A large number of Jews returned to Egypt after the destruction of Jerusalem, together with the reluctant Jeremiah (Jer 43:1-44:30). So great were the numbers of Jews in Alexandria at the time of Ptolemy I that he granted them a separate quarter of the city so that they might not be hindered in the observance of their own laws. Eventually the Jews made up 40% of the population of the city.

The Jews developed trade links with Ethiopia, too. Many of the local people were converted to Judaism. They possessed the entire Old Testament, apart from the book of Esther, but they did not have the *Talmud* or *Mishnah,* which would point to a date of conversion some time in the first century BC. The story of the conversion of the Ethiopian eunuch to Christianity in Acts 8:26-40 illustrates the religious links that existed with that country.

Jewish contacts extended to Europe, too. By 400 BC there were Jewish colonies in the area of the Middle Danube, north of the Black Sea, and even in Yugoslavia. The growth of the Greek influence in the Eastern Mediterranean caused a westward expansion of the Jews. In the course of the third and second centuries BC its effects became marked, leading to a major cultural rift between the Jews of the diaspora and those of Israel.

By the year 1 BC, the Jewish population in the world was probably about 8 million, compared with a total world population of 170 million. More than 2 million Jews lived in Judea, and more than a million each in Egypt, Syria, Asia Minor, and Persia.[4] Even Rome was said to have 50,000 Jews. No wonder Josephus wrote: 'It is hard to find a place in the habitable earth that has not admitted this tribe of men, and is not possessed by it.'[5]

Relevance of the Diaspora
Scattered amongst the nations, the Jews organised their

social and religious life in such a way as to allow themselves to maintain their existence as a distinct people. The religion of the Jews exercised a powerful influence upon the people among whom they were living, and many became proselytes. Two significant developments occurred during the diaspora which strengthened the religious life of the people in the dispersion.

The Synagogue

The origins of the synagogue are lost in obscurity. Some Jewish scholars find reference to the establishment of the synagogue in Ezekiel 11:16 (K J V) where the expression 'little sanctuary' is used. Whatever the origin, the synagogue pattern was of great importance throughout the Jewish world.

By the time of Christ, the number of synagogues in Jerusalem may have been as many as 480.[6] It seems likely that each of the synagogues served the distinct needs and interests of a specific segment of the Jewish community in the city. For example, Acts 6:9 refers to the 'synagogue of the Freedmen'. The synagogue was never regarded as a rival of the temple in Jerusalem, but a centre for the social life of the religious community. The synagogue had a variety of functions. It served as a social centre for the community — slaves were freed; honours were presented; hospitality was offered to strangers who needed accommodation. It was also a centre of moral and religious education for the community and became a meeting place for Jews and Gentiles — here there were no prohibitions as at the temple. The Gentiles could enter and listen to the teaching. The synagogue was also a centre of charity to those in need — the Pharisees collected funds to give to widows and orphans from both Jewish and proselyte families.

Thus the synagogue became a wonderfully adaptive structure suitable for all cultures; it became the bridge across which the people of God could share their faith with others, making possible the transition from Gentile to Jew.

As the Jews were scattered among the nations and were involved in trading, it was only to be expected that they would learn the language of the local people. Although they kept their distinct identity, gradually the Jewish communities became more fluent in the local language than in their native Hebrew. The vigorous Greek culture in the West influenced many of the Jews in various ways. These Hellenistic Jews adopted the Greek language, and many of the customs of the Greeks, much to the disgust of the more orthodox Hebrew-speaking Jews.

The fact that so many of the Jews began to speak Greek, and the growing number of proselytes could not speak Hebrew, led to translation of the Scriptures into Greek and the production of a version known as the *Septuagint*. Similar translations were to be made in other languages, but it was the Septuagint that became the missionary Bible of the young Church.

A means of effective communication was now established between the people of Israel and the nations of the world. The insularity of Israel was broken, and a bridge established for the communication of God's revelation to all peoples.

Jewish Proselytism

The synagogue and the translated Scriptures stimulated the interest of many people disillusioned with their traditional polytheistic religions. The ethical, monotheistic teaching of the Jews appealed to the Greeks, even though they were repelled by the practice of circumcision. Gentile enquirers were always welcomed in the synagogue, but men could not become full members of the community until they had been circumcised.

The central core of the synagogue community in the first century consisted of both ethnic Jews, and Gentile 'proselytes', the men of whom were circumcised. (See figure 12:1.) It was the act of circumcision that was the great criterion for determining the full sincerity of the Gentile convert. Many Gentile men would hesitate at becoming a full member of the Synagogue community because of this

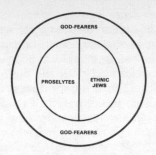

Fig 12:1

Social Groupings in the Synagogue
at the Time of Christ

issue and preferred to remain God-fearers. They would, however, often have their sons circumcised according to Jewish law. Women, of course, would not have this difficulty, and this could explain why there were more women converts. It was amongst these God-fearers that Paul was to later find much response, and this was therefore to highlight the whole issue of whether Gentile converts to Christianity should be circumcised.

The favourable attitude of the Old Testament to the foreigner (*ger*) was recognised by the Pharisees. The rights of a proselyte was therefore carefully guarded. If a proselyte was robbed, restitution was made according to the formula of Numbers 5:7, 8 — the principal plus an additional 20%. The Pharisees approved of making proselytes and actively encouraged it by making reference to the great men of the Old Testament who were proselytes. As one writer said: 'The righteous among the Gentiles are priests of God. The saints of all nations have a share in the world to come.'[7]

The convert to Judaism was identified not only with the Jewish religion, but with the people of Israel themselves. This, however, required the converts to take upon themselves the whole of the Jewish culture. (This was to become a major issue for the early Church and will be discussed in chapter 19.)

121

During the 1st century BC there was much active proselytism by the Jewish leaders. Writers such as Philo in Alexandria were writing apologetic works directed towards the Gentiles, and even using their own thought patterns. The coming of Christ coincided with the high-point of Jewish missionary activity. The development of Christianity did not hinder this effort, and proselytism continued until anti-Jewish legislation finally brought it to an end in the fifth century.[7]

The Rebuke of Jesus
In the light of this unparalleled missionary effort, Jesus' rebuke of the Pharisees becomes important. Why did Jesus condemn the Pharisees? What have modern missionaries to learn?

> Woe to you, teachers of the Law and Pharisees, you hypocrites! You travel over land and sea to win a single convert, and when he becomes one, you make him twice as much a son of hell as you are.

(Matt 23:15)

It is important to recognise that Jesus is not criticising the missionary zeal of the Pharisees. He is rebuking them for their example and the instruction they give to their converts. Jesus saw the kingdom of God as bringing men under the rule of God. The Pharisees were more concerned at bringing the convert under the rule of the man-made laws of Judaism. It was not the purpose of the Pharisees merely to change a Gentile into a Jew; no, he must become the same legalistic, hair-splitting Pharisee as themselves. As Jesus implies, soon this new convert would even outdo the Pharisee in bigotry, for it is a fact that new converts frequently outdo their teachers in becoming fanatically devoted to the new faith.

The term 'proselyte' comes from the Greek word meaning 'I come near, I approach'. As we have seen it was the word used of a Gentile who was circumcised and had adopted the Jewish faith. As the word was almost exclusively used to describe a convert to Judaism, the Early

Church did not apply the word but spoke of Gentiles becoming 'disciples', 'saints', or later 'Christians'.

During the last century the term 'proselytising' took on a derogatory meaning. The liberal theologians rejected the word because they disliked any radical form of Christian conversion. The term is now used by both evangelical and liberal theologians as the opposite of true Christian conversion. 'Proselytism is not something absolutely different from witness: it is the corruption of witness. When cajolery, bribery, undue pressure, or intimidation is used — subtly or openly — to bring about seeming conversion.'[9] Perhaps the contrast between the two ways is best illustrated thus:

Pharisee	Jesus
↓	↓
Man-made laws	Law of the Spirit
↓	↓
Hypocrisy	Sincerity
↓	↓
Self-righteousness	Salvation by Faith
↓	↓
'Son of hell'	'Son of God'

And Matthew in verse 23:15 shows that the test of mission is not the zeal with which one pursues another to join the Church, but rather what one makes of them after they have been won.

Discussion Questions

1 How far should our church buildings reflect the flexible usage found in the ancient synagogues?

2 All of us have some practices which we do, or don't do, for religious reasons. Some may not choose to read a newspaper on Sunday, whilst others may choose not to play football, or watch television. What activities do you engage in that may make yourself or others uncomfortable? Which of these would you encourage a young convert to follow or not to follow, and why?

3 Why is Bible translation important in Christian mission?

Recommended Reading

Nicholas de Lange, *Atlas of the Jewish World* (Phaidon Press: Oxford, 1984).

E A Martens, *Plot and Purpose in the Old Testament* (IVP: Leicester, 1981).

Footnotes

1   John T Seamands, *Tell It Well: Communicating the Gospel across Cultures* (Beacon Hill Press: Kansas City, 1981) p 95.

2   Richard H DeRidder, *Discipling the Nations* (Baker Book House: Grand Rapids, 1975) p 64.

4   DeRidder, *op cit*.

5   Flavius Josephus, *The Antiquities of the Jews* (Pickering & Inglis: London, 1960) p 390.

6   DeRidder, *op cit* p 79.

7   DeRidder, *op cit* pp 99 (quote from Sanh. XIII, 2).

8   Jacques Bloches, 'Mission — And Proselytism', in Harold Lindsell *The Church's Worldwide Mission* (Word Books: Waco, 1966) p 112.

9   Jacques Bloches, *op cit* pp 111-123.

13

THE KING AND THE KINGDOM

A Paraphrase from Philippians 2

Let your cross-cultural perspectives have as their vantage point the life of Christ. For Christ belonged to a celestial culture, where he fit in perfectly enough to rank with the best.

But he put that aside and entered a terrestrial culture, carrying with him no extra baggage, no sense of superiority, no chauvinism, no presumptions. He joined its peoples, and became one of them until he not only could see from their point of view, but could live their kind of life.

His identification was so complete that he died for their cause. God noticed, and honoured the venture by making Christ the universal focal point, in whom all people can have common vision.[1]

The period of silence following the last of the prophets left Israel expecting something new. They anticipated a coming king who would burst upon the stage of world history to establish his Kingdom. Here would be a king who would accomplish the mission of God for Israel (see the section entitled *The Messiah*, ch 11, p108-109).

In turning to the New Testament one must recognise that the 'new thing' about to come to fruition had already commenced in the Old Testament. The New Testament does not do away with the Old but adds to it, both in quantity and quality. As Johannes Blauw has written, 'Of essential importance for the construction of a theology of mission is

125

that both the unity and diversity of the Old Testament and New Testament must be kept in mind.'[2]

The Mystery of the Kingdom

Old Testament Concept

After the fall of Jerusalem, the idea of a Davidic kingdom was enlarged by the apocalyptic concept of the kingdom. In this view God was seen as breaking into human history to establish his Kingdom. The prophecy in Daniel 2 is an impressive example of this teaching. The king dreams of a huge image made up of different layers of materials which is finally destroyed by a stone. The interpretation given later in the chapter is that the image represents the successive nations which would dominate the course of world history. The stone represents the coming of the kingdom of God as a single great event: a mighty manifestation of God's power which would sweep away the wicked kingdoms of human sovereignty and would fill the earth with righteousness.

The Voice

It was in the midst of this apocalyptic expectation that John the Baptist came as a voice crying in the wilderness. Here was a man like Elijah! Here was a man calling the Jews into the wilderness (the traditional place of encounter with God and renewal) to repent: 'Repent, for the kingdom of heaven is near!' (Matt 3:2)

John was only a forerunner pointing to Jesus who was the coming King. It may well have been that even John had his doubts as to whether Jesus was the Messiah. The fact that he sent some of his disciples to ask Jesus his identity highlights an important aspect of Christ's mission. John's disciples ask the crucial question, 'Are you one who was to come, or should we expect someone else' (Matt 11:3)

Jesus did not reply by giving a direct answer to their question but points instead to his actions (Matt 11:4-7). The sick were healed, the dead were raised, and good news was preached to the poor. The era of the Kingdom was signified by healing, deliverance and restoration. A new order had broken into the world, and the miracles were 'signs' of its presence.

The old order was under threat by the invasion of the new. For many Western people the notion of the supernatural world is one difficult to fully comprehend, but the Bible clearly assumes its reality and considers the coming of Christ as an encounter with Satan and his forces. The picture given is one of a conflict between two opposing kingdoms. 'It is rather by means of God's power that I drive out demons, and this proves that the kingdom of God has already come to you' (Luke 11:20). 'But if I drive out demons by the finger of God, then the kingdom of God has come to you. The Son of God appeared for this very reason, to destroy what the Devil had done' (I John 3:8).

The Teaching of Jesus

Throughout the teaching of Jesus the element of mystery concerning the nature of the kingdom is consistent. In Matthew 13 and Mark 4 Jesus tells a series of parables concerning the Kingdom. Although the stories are drawn from everyday experiences of the people, the central truth is called 'the mystery' of the Kingdom.

In modern English, the word mystery bears the connotation of something which is deep, profound and difficult. However, in the Scriptures the word takes on almost a technical meaning, being used to indicate that which has been kept secret for long ages but is now disclosed (see Rom 16:25-26). A mystery is a purpose of God which has been hidden but is finally disclosed in a new revelation of his work.

The old era lasted until John came, but then something radically new commenced with Jesus. Jesus' challenge to accept unconditionally the rule of God for one's life was so radical that it could only be described by using the language of force: 'The Law and the Prophets were proclaimed until John. Since that time, the Good News of the Kingdom of God is being preached, and everyone is forcing his way into it' (Luke 16:16). The supreme mystery of the Kingdom is the fact that the King is the Messiah, Jesus Christ.

Message of the Kingdom

The Greek word *basileia* (kingdom) can mean both the geographical area over which a king reigns as well as the exercise of kingly authority. In the Gospels it is clearly the latter sense in which the word is used. The Kingdom consists of all that falls under the rule and sovereignty of God.

Signs of the Kingdom

In the Wheaton Document of 1983,[3] considerable discussion was given by evangelical scholars as to the nature of the signs of the Kingdom. Jesus did more than preach the Kingdom but demonstrated its reality with 'signs' which were evident to the people. What are the signs for the presence of the Kingdom in our age? The Wheaton Document lists seven, approximately in the order in which they appear in the Gospels:

1 Jesus in the midst of his people (Luke 17:21; Matt 18:20)

2 The preaching of the Gospel of the Kingdom (Luke 17:21)

3 Exorcism (Matt 12:29; Mark 3:27)

4 Healing and nature miracles (Luke 22; John 14:12)

5 Miracle of conversion and new birth (I Thess 1:9, 10)

6 Manifestation of a Christlike character (Gal 5:22, 23)

7 Suffering (I Pet 2:21)

The majority of the items would be agreed by all, but the matters of exorcism, healing and nature miracles have long been debated. Many holding to a dispensationalist view have argued that miracles only occurred during the period of the Early Church. This was to enable the young Church to become established, but now, they say, the Church is founded upon the Word of God — the Bible.

Although one must recognise that some leading Christian scholars have held this view, it contradicts a major principle of biblical exposition: that biblical truth is that obtained from the plain reading of Scriptures. If one denies the reality of miracles today, it becomes a short step to the denial of the relevance of other aspects of New Testament teaching today. Just because we do not experience the reality of miracles in our churches and lives, we cannot assume that miracles do not happen today. The testimony of many, especially in the Third World, is that the miraculous does occur today, and an increasing number in Western nations are discovering this reality.[4]

Both the words and works of Jesus are the beginning of a new age – the kingdom of God. The casting out of demons signals God's invasion of the kingdom of Satan and foretells his future destruction. The healing of the sick witnesses to the end of all suffering (Rev 21:4). The stilling of the storm shows the power of the Kingdom to be greater than even that of the forces of nature.

The Coming of the Kingdom

The apocalyptic expectation of the kingdom of God was envisaged by many Jews in the first century, and many sought to bring it into reality. A comparison of their various approaches not only focusses our attention on the method employed by Jesus himself, but allows us to consider our own methods of mission.

The Essenes

Of all these groups, the most well known is that of the Dead Sea community. Like many others scattered around Israel at that time, this community consisted of orthodox groups seeking to hold on to their traditions by isolating themselves from society. Their mission was withdrawal, and throughout the history of the Church such an option has frequently been exercised.

Zealots

The revolutionary option was strong in the first century as many dreamed of a new Davidic Kingdom with the son of David as its King. Many zealot groups existed among the Jews, but Jesus avoided the revolutionary option even when the people wanted to make him King. Jesus did not, however, avoid confronting the corrupt religious system of his

129

day. In the temple he turns over the tables of the money changers and the stools of those who sold pigeons (Matt 21:12). This was no impassioned outburst, but the King entering into his Father's house: 'Zeal for your house consumes me' (Ps 69:9).

While rejecting violence, the ministry of Jesus still had political repercussions. The outcome of his Kingdom was not limited to a supernatural or eschatological realm but had imminent implications, as Yoder comments:

> Jesus was not just a moralist whose teachings had some political implications; he was not primarily a teacher of spirituality whose ministry unfortunately was seen in a political light . . . , Jesus was, in his divinely mandated prophethood, priesthood, and kinghood, the bearer of a new possibility, social and therefore political relationships.[5]

The Pharisees

The Pharisees were a lay movement who were dedicated to the fulfilment of the traditional legal system. They held that the Exile was a result of the Jews' failure to obey the Torah (the Mosaic Law). They were therefore fanatical in their zeal to obey the Torah in every respect, even to the extent of adding instructions as to how one should obey the Law. Orthodox and proud of their own personal achievements, the Pharisees tended to be exclusive and critical of others.

The Jesus Model

Jesus rejected each of these models for mission and pursued his mission in the spirit of the suffering servant so clearly presented in what several theologians have called the *Nazareth Manifesto*.

> Here is my servant, whom I have chosen,
> the one I love, in whom I delight;
> I will put my Spirit on him,
> and he will proclaim justice to the nations.
> He will not quarrel or cry out;
> no one will hear his voice in the streets.

A bruised reed he will not break,
and a smouldering wick he will not snuff out,
till he leads justice to victory.
In his name the nations will put their hope.

(Matt 12:18-20; Isa 42:2-3)

The mission of this King was accomplished with an attitude that differed totally from that of others. He was humble, self-effacing, and non-triumphalistic. He came as a servant willing to do the will of the Father even though it meant a costly identification with human nature and experience. He was also gentle and supportive of the weak. He helped those in need, healed the sick, and comforted the sorrowing. And he was tenacious in fulfilling the will of his Father. Thus Jesus not only commanded his followers to go and make disciples of all nations, but he gave them an example to follow. Many heroes of Christian mission can give good examples of how mission should be accomplished, but the supreme model for our mission to a broken world must be the King himself. This fact alone should drive the missionary to study the life of Jesus in greater depth: 'Peace be with you! As the Father has sent me, I am sending you' (John 20:21).

Discussion Questions

1 Do you agree with the view that miracles occur today? Would you agree that the responsibility for allowing the miracle-working power of God to operate lies within ourselves?

2 Some writers have argued that there is healing in the atonement (Exod 15:26; Isa 53:5). Do you think that children of God have the right to claim healing for themselves? If so, how can this be reconciled with the occasions when healing does not come?

3 Read the passage in which Jesus sends out the Twelve (Matt 10:5-15), and consider how these instructions challenge your own understanding of evangelism.

131

Recommended Reading

George Eldon Ladd, *The Gospel of the Kingdom* (Paternoster Press: Exeter, 1959).

Monica Hill, editor, *Entering the Kingdom* (MARC Europe: London, 1986).

John Bright, *The Kingdom of God* (Abingdon Press: Nashville, 1953).

Michael Griffiths, *The Example of Jesus* (Hodder & Stoughton: London, 1985).

Norman Anderson, *The Teaching of Jesus* (Hodder & Stoughton: London, 1983).

John Wimber, *Power Evangelism* (Hodder & Stoughton: London, 1985).

Arthur P Johnston, 'The Kingdom in Relation to the Church and the World', *In Word and Deed*, Ed Bruce J Nicholls (1985) pp 109-134.

Footnotes

1 J Daniel Hess, *From the Other's Point of View* (Herald Press: Ontario, 1980), p 256.

2 Johannes Blauw, *The Missionary Nature of the Church* (Lutterworth Press: London, 1962) p 106.

3 'Wheaton '83 Statement, Social Transformation: 'The Church in Response to Human Need', *Transformation* Vol 1, No 1 (1984): pp 23-28.

4 See John Wimber, *Power Evangelism: Signs and Wonders Today* (Hodder & Stoughton: London, 1985).

5 John Howard Yoder, *Politics of Jesus* (Eerdmans: Grand Rapids, 1972) p 62.

14

THE MISSION OF
THE KINGDOM

A new missionary to Nigeria was deeply thrilled when he got a land grant from the local king so that he could begin to build a mission hospital. Once the building began, he started each workday with Bible study and prayer for his work crew. Long before the hospital was ready to function, all his workmen had 'accepted Christ', and the missionary felt that even the construction time had been an evangelistic success.

Once the building was complete all the workmen returned to their respective home villages, and the missionary began organising a series of evangelistic tours through some of those same villages. To his complete amazement he found that his 'converts' were contentedly tending idol shrines in their home villages. When he confronted them with what to him was a gross incongruity with their confession of faith as Christians, they in turn expressed their surprise at his abysmal ignorance: surely he knew that at the mission they had prayed to owo (God) because they saw that he was the one who had power there, but he was not in charge here in their home villages. Here they had to pray to their 'deity that owned this area.' 'If we try to pray to your mission God here, the local deity would be very, very unhappy and make too much trouble for everyone,' they affirmed with conviction.[1]

The coming of the King is the most important single fact with regards to the kingdom of God. There are two aspects of the Kingdom which are of importance for us to consider further. The first relates to the scope of the Kingdom. From Jesus' viewpoint, does the Kingdom include the Gentiles, or is it exclusive to the Jews only? Secondly, what is the nature of the mission of the Kingdom?

Jesus' Mission — to Jews or Gentiles?

Although Jesus is always gracious to Gentiles, he makes some very surprising utterances with regard to them. To a distressed Canaanite mother, he says: 'I was sent only to the lost sheep of Israel' (Matt 15:24). When sending out his disciples he gave them the perplexing command, 'Do not go among the Gentiles or enter any town of the Samaritans. Go, rather, to the lost sheep of Israel' (Matt 10:5, 6). The complexity is increased by the fact that Jesus, on the other hand, also informed the disciples that they would 'be brought before governors and kings as witnesses to them and to the Gentiles' (Matt 10:18).

It is not satisfactory to say that one should ignore these words concerning the lost sheep of the people of Israel in the light of the clear command to make disciples of all nations. These limitations were for a limited period but were an important aspect of the whole mission of Jesus. Jesus was conscious that he came into the world for a particular task to fulfil the mission of Israel.

To Israel Only?

God's call to Abraham was to be the father of a great nation which would ultimately bring about the restoration of all the nations (Gen 12:1-4). The covenant with Israel was not just for her salvation but that she may be the first fruits of an enlightening of the nations. Israel had failed to do this. Christ came to be God's Shepherd, to gather around him God's people. It would be through the restoration of the servant nation that all the nations of the world would be blessed.

Christ's ministry was defined in terms which exactly corresponded to the terms of God's universal covenant and Israel's election. He was to live his life and perform his saving work in terms of the judgement God pronounced on him for the sake of, and in the place of Israel. In working for the salvation of Israel, Jesus worked for the salvation of the whole world: '. . . salvation is from the Jews' (John 4:22).

The Inclusion of the Gentiles

DeRidder[2] has shown the attitude of Jesus to the Gentiles is further illustrated by the cleansing of the temple. This well known incident is placed by Matthew at the end of Christ's ministry (Matt 21:1-11). Jewish sources say that the money changers used to set up their tables three weeks before the Passover, the time when the temple tax fell due. The merchants set their stalls up in the court of the Gentiles. This was the only part of the temple to which the Gentiles had access, and therefore the only area of the temple in which they could pray.

When Jesus turned over the tables and put the merchants out of the temple he was not just making a plea for a more spiritual worship but demanding that room is made in God's house for the Gentiles to come and worship: 'My house will be called a house of prayer for all nations' (Mark 11:17).

This act of Jesus was not a demonstration of uncontrolled anger, but an act of the King coming to his Father's house to set it to rights, and to provide a proper place for the Gentiles in it. The very words used by Jesus are from Isaiah (ch 56), which is one of the clearest demonstrations of God's universal concern for all nations. The Gentiles would be drawn to the temple, as was prophesied by Isaiah.

Jesus was to give added significance to this prophecy by relating the temple to his own body (John 2:19-22). The destruction of the temple and the influx of the Gentiles into the temple became inseparably linked. The kingdom of God would not mean the triumph of Israel over the nations but the inclusion of the nations. Earthly distinctions would be abolished: 'For he himself is our peace, who has made the two one and has destroyed the barrier, the dividing wall of hostility' (Eph 2:14).

The importance of this fact for Christian mission is self-evident. DeRidder underlines it: 'The implications are tremendous for the Christian mission. No one may under any circumstance claim to have Christ on his side or for himself alone, be the man Jew or Gentile, man or woman, Westerner, African, or Asian.'[3]

The few Gentiles of whom one reads in the Gospels always approach Jesus, never the reverse. However, to this 'centripetal' mission would eventually be added the 'centrifugal' aspect – reaching out to all peoples. (See figure 5:1, p 56.) Acts chapter 2 sees the initiation of the outreach of the Church which is continuing to this day.

The Church's Mission – in Word or Deed?

The second question to be considered with regards to the mission of the kingdom concerns the very nature of the missionary task itself. A dichotomy is often perceived between that aspect of mission relating to a verbal proclamation of the Gospel, and that related to social concern. Is such a dichotomy necessary?

During the history of the Protestant missionary movement, people have shown every possible attitude to evangelism and social concern. William Carey, for example, did not draw any apparent distinction between the two. In addition to his preaching and Bible translation in India, he established a university, a printing press, and a botanical garden.

With the rise of liberal scholarship, emphasis was placed upon social action as part of what came to be known as 'the social gospel'. In reaction to this, many evangelicals swung to the position of rejecting all social action, apart from medical work and education. They considered their mission was evangelism alone.

During the 1960's, however, evangelicals began to strive for a new balance. John Stott[4] greatly helped the formulation of a more biblical relationship, and Christians from the Third World added their voices. Samuel Escobar spoke of the Western evangelicals, 'edited' Gospel, strong in the Cross and its private appropriation, but weak in the Kingdom and all its social implications. 'Christian service is not optional . . . it is the mark of new life: "You will know them by their fruits" . . . So to discuss whether we should evangelise or promote social action is worthless. They go together. They are inseparable.'[5]

It has become clear that what has been needed is not just an improvement of the balance between evangelism and social action, but a new conceptual framework for fusing the various elements together. In the ministry of Jesus we perceive no dichotomy but a meeting of the needs of people where they were. When he sent out his disciples he gave them an integrated mission: 'As you go, preach this message: "The kingdom of heaven is near!" Heal the sick, raise the dead, cleanse those who have leprosy, drive out demons' (Matt 10:7).

Neither Jesus nor the apostles differentiated evangelism from social action as two different responses to two different sets of human needs, but responded to the total man with his integrated needs and aspirations. Their words and their deeds were consistent with the fact of the coming Kingdom.

The tension between evangelism and social action has led to five major positions. The first argues that social action is a distraction from evangelism. This view rightly tries to give a proper emphasis upon the spiritual needs of a person. Man is basically a sinner who needs to be saved. However, it easily allows neglect of the fact that man is not just an immaterial soul but is part of a living society. The weakness of this view arises in its lack of recognition of the world situation as the arena in which faith and obedience are demonstrated.

Other people have regarded social action primarily as a means to evangelism. In this second view priority is given to evangelism and the winning of converts, in which social action may often be a useful preliminary. Development programmes may be the ways in which evangelistic agencies enter a country hostile to Christians. However, such intentions must be considered carefully lest they misrepresent the primary aims.

A third view is that social action is a manifestation of evangelism. Social action is seen as a natural expression of the very nature of the Gospel. Bavinck agrees that medicine and education are more than just a means of creating an opportunity for preaching. He writes: 'If these services are motivated by the proper love and compassion then they cease to be simply preparation and that very moment become preaching.'[6]

The fourth view is the traditional position of the social gospel — i.e. that social action is equivalent to evangelism — and will not be considered any further at this point.

The fifth view of evangelism and social action fuses the two elements together into what has become known as 'wholistic mission'.[7] The Wheaton '83 conference sought to deal with this relationship, and turned to a Kingdom model for the answer.[8]

The Kingdom Model

The Kingdom model provides a much more adequate view of the nature of the mission of the Church. With the coming of the Kingdom an additional dimension is added to the cultural mandate — that of the 'redemptive mandate' (see figure 1:3, page 20). The redemption mandate enlarges and gives the cultural mandate a greater depth and significance.

The community of the Kingdom should constitute a radical challenge to the old order. It is a new way of looking at the world with new values, new moral standards, and a new way of life. These issues will spill over into every era of life and into society as a whole — commerce, industry, law, education, and government.

To apply an artificial distinction between spiritual and physical needs will lead to a narrow view of the Kingdom. As Michael Cassidy has said: 'I used to say that we just have to get men and women converted to Jesus Christ, and socio-political issues will sort themselves out. But, I keep finding that the most "theologically converted" people are the ones who entrench the status quo.'[9] Jesus, on the other hand, used three very telling metaphors concerning the nature of the Kingdom life within the world: salt, light, and yeast (Matt 5:13-16). Each of these elements dynamically penetrates the old order. Salt soaks into the food; light shines into darkness; yeast ferments within the dough. In turn, the Kingdom community will penetrate the old society bringing cultural transformation that will bring wholeness to the people.

The Incarnation – Pattern for Kingdom Life

The Kingdom model was supremely demonstrated by the King himself. The Son of God, willing to identify with humanity, became a man. As the Willowbank Report has stated this is 'the most spectacular instance of cultural identification in the history of mankind, since by his Incarnation the Son became a first-century Galilean Jew'.[10]

In the Incarnation, the Word did not merely become human, but became a particular human being in space and time. Jesus intimately involved himself with the Jewish people. For him it meant a Jewish lifestyle with Jewish customs within a Jewish family. Even so, he remained pure and holy, and was a living demonstration of the nature of God being lived out in Jewish culture. This could not be achieved without immense cost; identification required renunciation.

Jesus intended his people's mission to be modelled on his own: 'As the Father has sent me, I am sending you,' he said (John 20:21). This brings tremendous implications for cross-cultural witness. Faced with the task of identifying with the people to whom he goes, the missionary must renounce much of his own cultural tradition. The incarnation teaches that identification is possible without loss of personal integrity.

Discussion Questions

1 How would you respond to the argument that the use of social action as a means of entering a country hostile to Christians, hints of hypocrisy?

2 Although one may develop a *theoretical* model for an integrated approach to mission, there are many complex *practical* implications. What advice would you give to a busy missionary doctor as to his priorities?

3 Does the fact that physical need can be more graphically illustrated than spiritual need cause us to have an inbalance in our priorities?

4 List some of the incidents in the life of Christ when he

refused to conform to the Jewish way of life. Where does the limit come in cultural identification?

Recommended Reading

Tom Sine, *The Mustard Seed Conspiracy* (MARC Europe: London, 1985).

'The Willowbank Report — Gospel and Culture', *Lausanne Occasional Papers* No 2 (1978).

Lesslie Newbigin, *The Open Secret* (Eerdmans Publishing Co: Grand Rapids, USA, 1981).

Bruce J Nicholls, Ed, *In Word and Deed — Evangelism and Social Responsibility* (Paternoster Press Ltd: Exeter, 1985).

Footnotes

1 Jacob Loewen, 'Which God do Missionaries Preach?' *Missiology: An International Review* Vol XIV, No 1 (January 1986) pp 3-19.

2 Richard H DeRidder, *Discipling the Nations* (Baker Book House: Grand Rapids, 1975) pp 155-161.

3 *ibid* p 160.

4 John Stott, *Walk in His Shoes* (IVP: Leicester, 1975).

5 Samuel Escobar, 'Evangelism & Man's Search for Freedom, Justice & Fulfilment', in *Let the Earth hear His Voice* (World Wide Publications: Minneapolis, 1975) pp 303-326.

6 J H Bavinck, *An Introduction to the Science of Mission* (The Presbyterian & Reformed Publishing Co: Philadelphia, 1960) p 113.

7 See *Partnership*, No 5, Sept 1976.

8 Tom Sine, *The Church in Response to Human Need* (MARC International: Monrovia, 1983).

9 See *Partnership*, No 5, Sept 1976.

10 *Explaining the Gospel in Today's World* (Scripture Union: London, 1978) p 17.

15

THE GOSPEL
MANDATE

As we talked about evangelism and a message for India, I asked: 'When you preach in India, what do you emphasise?' 'Do you preach to them the love of God?'

'No,' he said, 'not particularly. The Indian mind is so polluted that if you talk to them about love they think mainly of sex life. You do not talk to them much about the love of God.'

'Well,' I said, 'do you talk to them about the wrath of God and the judgement of God?'

'No, this is not my emphasis,' he remarked, 'they are used to that. All the gods are mad anyway. It makes no difference to them if there is one more who is angry!'

'What do you talk to them about? Do you preach Christ and Him crucified?' I guessed.

'No,' he replied. 'They would think of Him as a poor martyr who helplessly died.'

'What is your emphasis? Do you talk to them about eternal life?' 'No,' he said. 'If you talk to them about eternal life, the Indian thinks of transmigration. He wants to get away from it. Don't emphasise eternal life.'

'What then is your message?'

'I have never yet failed to get a hearing if I talk to them about forgiveness of sins and peace and rest in your hearts. That's the product that sells well. Soon they ask me how they can get it. Having won their hearing I lead them on to the Saviour who alone can meet their deepest needs.'[1]

The mission of Israel was basically one in which people would be drawn to the nation. To this centripetal motion Jesus was to give to his disciples a new commission to go out into the whole world. It is therefore not surprising that the Great Commission has been so influential in the modern missionary movement; however, this has not always been the case. The Reformers, and the majority of the theologians of the seventeenth century held that the Commission was binding only upon the apostles. When the apostles died the Commission died with them, and so it had no significance for the contemporary world.

In 1792, Carey published his book, *An enquiry into the Obligation of Christians to Use Means for the Conversion of the Heathen*,[2] arguing that Christ's command in Matthew 28 was binding on Christians of all ages, not just upon the apostles. The command, he asserted, had not been repealed, and it therefore should be obeyed by the followers of Christ of every age. It may seem strange to many people today that Carey should have had such great difficulty in presenting his arguments, but this is because we take for granted the radical influence his views have had upon the twentieth-century view of mission. But in the light of the present rethinking of mission, it is valuable to consider the Great Commission. What does it have to say to today's Church? How does the Great Commission add to the cultural mandate? (See p20.)

The Chronological Setting

The Great Commission is not just a single statement found in Matthew 28 but consists of five statements found in the first five books of the New Testament. Each statement adds elements to the total Commission.

The first statement, in chronological order, is that found in John's Gospel (ch 20:19-23). The event occurs in the upper room where the frightened group of disciples have gathered. Here the resurrected Christ appears and speaks peace to them. He then goes on to show them his hands and his feet as evidence of his resurrection. It is at this time that he gives them the commission, 'As the Father has sent me, I am sending you.' Seeing his nail-marked hands must have impressed upon them that his mission entailed suffering,

142

and therefore so must theirs; however, immediately Jesus goes on to give them the promise of the Holy Spirit.

The second statement occurs after the incident on the Emmaus road when Jesus suddenly appeared to the disciples. (Luke 24:36-48). This passage is an expansion of the passage in John. However, reference is here made to the fact that Jesus' ministry does not stand alone but comes within the whole context of the Old Testament Scriptures. This is a point stressed by Peters when he writes: 'The Great Commission is not an isolated command arbitarily imposed upon Christianity. It is the logical summation and natural overflow of the character of God as he is revealed in the Scriptures, of the missionary purpose and thrust of God as unfolded in the Old Testament.'[3]

Mark 16 provides the third statement of the Commission. It is only found in the 'longer ending' (verses 14-18) and shows many parallels with the text of Matthew. One additional factor is the emphasis on believers being given the power to perform miracles.

The fourth statement is that in Matthew which will be considered in greater detail in the next section. The final statement is that in the book of Acts 1:6-8 just prior to the Ascension of our Lord. The universal scope of the missionary task is here clearly stated, even though the disciples still seemed to be confused as to the role of Israel and the Kingdom (Acts 1:6).

The Authority of Jesus

A major aspect of the Great Commission is the emphasis that Jesus places upon his authority. This is vitally important, because unless Jesus has such authority how can he give such a command? This is a kingly command which assumes that he is Lord over all peoples. If Jesus is not the King, his Commission is presumptious and without foundation. If he is King, then the whole of life ought to be subject to his royal authority. The fact that God is King is the heart of the Gospel message.

The authority of the missionary lies therefore in the very person of Christ. If Jesus is the King of God's Kingdom then the missionary has the right, even the duty, to go to all people. If he is not King, then the missionary has no right to seek to take his religious ideas to others. Is Jesus Lord? This is the vital question.

Throughout the Gospels people were amazed at the authority of Jesus (Matt 7:29; 9:6, 8; 10:1). In his Commission Jesus stresses that all authority (Greek *pasa exousia*) in heaven and earth has been given unto him. Clearly his authority has been enlarged, for 'God placed all things under his feet and appointed him to be head over everything for the church' (Eph 1:22).

Even so, there is a sense in which Christ's authority is not over all. 'We know that we are children of God, and that the whole world is under the control of the evil one' (I John 5:19). Paul speaks of 'principalities and powers', and of Satan as being the 'god of this age' (II Cor 4:4). How can Christ claim universal authority if the whole world still lies in Satan's power?

The answer is that Jesus is in fact King over the redeemed people of his Kingdom, while it is only by right that he is presently King over the world — a right still challenged by the usurper. A time will come when Satan will eventually have to acknowledge the Lordship of Christ, and at that time 'every knee will bow'.

It is important to recognise the relationship between these two perspectives. To assume that all authority has in fact been given to Christ can lead one to seriously neglect the presence of evil powers in the world. On the other hand, to limit the reign of Christ can lead one to dismiss the world as being beyond redemption. These two views must be kept in balance.

The Task of the Disciple

The actual task given by Jesus is summed up in verse 19 of the Matthew passage: 'Therefore go and make disciples of all nations, baptising them . . . and teaching them to obey everything I have commanded you.' The sentence in the Greek is made up of three participle clauses modifying the main verb which is *matheteuo* ('make disciples'). The emphasis in the passage is therefore placed on the task of making disciples. Going, baptising, and teaching are the necessary aspects to making disciples. The command 'go' is placed at the beginning of the sentence both in the Greek and in the English because it logically precedes the ultimate task of making disciples.

The central task is that of making disciples, and in this the person of Christ is central. A disciple is one who places himself under the authority of another and willingly accepts the person as being his master. For the Christian, this amounts to placing himself under the reign of the King. A disciple is one who has a very personal relationship with his teacher, more than an apprentice — one who lives and works with the master. This is nowhere more clearly seen than in the disciples themselves, who lived with Jesus for three years. The master is the model whom they follow and whose teaching they not only accept intellectually, but put into practice in their own lives.

The word used in the parallel accounts in Luke (24:47) and Mark (16:15) is *kerusso* — 'preach'. This is a word meaning 'to herald', and so proclaim the Good News.[4] It has close association with the word *euangelizomai*, also frequently translated by the English word 'preach', but also the word 'evangelise'. Both words carry the concept of communicating good news. However, the aim is not merely to communicate a message, no matter how good that message may be, but to make disciples. The success of evangelism must not be measured against the yardstick of how many people have heard the Gospel, but rather how many people have been discipled.

The communication of Gospel facts is an essential part of this process, but the ultimate objective is that of making disciples. This process goes beyond conversion to an attitude of dedication to the King and submission to his reign. It involves a change of allegiance to Christ.

The two participles 'baptising' and 'teaching' describe the way in which the disciples are to be made. There are three aspects to the notion of baptism: submission, confession, and incorporation. The use of the phrase 'in the name'

145

seems to have links with the practice of heathen slaves being compelled to receive baptism on their entry into Jewish households. The slave was thus baptised into the family and a new set of social relations established, as well as a new submission to the head of the family. The parallel with Christian baptism is clearly apparent, where a new relationship is established between the baptised person and the Triune God.

Baptism also calls for a confession before the world of a change of allegiance. The person has transferred his loyalty from one god or hierarchy of gods, to the God of the Bible. Even today in most of the Third World this is how the act of baptism is regarded by non-Christians.

Baptism is also an act of incorporation into the Church. The change of allegiance means a leaving of one association and an entry into another. The Church is a community of people who have been 'called out' (*ecclesia*), and have come into a new association as the people of God.

The second element in making disciples is that of teaching (*didaskein*), the passing on of the teaching of Jesus Christ. However, such teaching must never be considered merely as the passing on of intellectual facts. Education must be a process of putting into practice all that Jesus commanded.

As to the question of what should be taught, one has to refer back to the whole text of Matthew. It is generally agreed that this Gospel was particularly constructed to facilitate its use as teaching material. The five main blocks of teaching provide the core of Christ's teaching.

1 Matt 5-7 Ethics of the Kingdom
2 Matt 10 Mission of the Kingdom
3 Matt 13 Growth of the Kingdom
4 Matt 18 Fellowship of the Kingdom
5 Matt 24, 25 Consummation of the Kingdom

The Great Commission draws all these strands together and sets them as the teaching material for discipling.

The Scope of the Commission

Three different words are used in the Great Commission concerning to whom the disciples should go. Matthew uses the phrase *panta ta ethna* — all the nations. The Greek word *ethna* is the root of the English word ethnic, signifying a race of people. When this phrase is used of the Gentiles it is used of all the peoples who do not belong to the chosen people. However, it does not refer to these peoples as a worldwide census of individuals, but rather as separate ethnic groups who, taken together, comprise mankind as a whole.

The book of Revelation provides a descriptive listing of the peoples of the world: 'every tribe and language and people and nation' (Rev 5:9; 7:9; 11:9; 13:7; 14:6). Language, race, culture, and national allegiance all go to describe the identity of a people. The divisions first formed at Babel have become an integral part of humankind like a vast cultural mosaic. It is to this multi-cultural situation that Christ calls his disciples to reach out with the Good News of the Kingdom.

This concept is taken further in Acts 1:8: 'you will be my witnesses in Jerusalem, and in all Judaea and Samaria, and to the ends of the earth.' The expanding circles are not just indicative of a widening geographical responsibility, but show a widening cultural concern. To include the Samaritans was an anathema to the Jews, and yet the concern of Christ was to all people, even to those despised by the Jews.

In Mark 16:15 he uses the word *kosmos* which has even wider connotations than that of *ethna*. Here the reference is to the whole inhabited world that God so loved that he sent his only Son. The word indicates an unqualified universalism including both Jews and Gentiles alike. It is this fallen *kosmos* that is in rebellion against God. When this *kosmos* is redeemed and comes under the reign of God it then becomes the kingdom of God.

The third phrase is one also used in Mark 16:15 *pase te ktisei* — to the whole creation. The scope is opened yet wider to the whole created order. God the Creator confronts his creatures with his purpose of having created them.

The Promise of Jesus

The Commission ends with a quite astonishing promise, 'I will be with you always, to the very end of the age.' The reassurance of the divine presence was a regular feature of commissioning in the Old Testament (e.g. Gen 17:4; 28:15; Exodus 4:11-12; Joshua 1:5-6, 9). Here it is Jesus who promises to be with his disciples through all difficulties until the end of the age. Blauw[5] argues that the promise has both a temporal and geographical element. It is a promise not only of divine presence, but also of divine activity in and through the people of God as they go to all people of every age.

The words of the Great Commission are not merely added comments to the Gospel records, but are the very high points of the purposes of God. As Dr O'Brian has written: 'These verses of Matthew 28 are among the most important words in the whole Gospel. They serve as the climax, integrally related to the purposes of Matthew as a whole.'[6]

Discussion Questions

1 Study the life of Christ, and find what principles he used to disciple his followers.

2 By what authority do missionaries have the right to seek to convert people to the Christian faith?

3 What are the principal facts that must be contained in the message of true evangelism?

Recommended Reading

Max Warren, *I Believe in the Great Commission* (Hodder & Stoughton: London, 1976).

Peter T O'Brian, 'The Great Commission of Matthew 28:18-20' *Evangelical Review of Theology* (Vol II, No 2, 1978) pp 254-67.

David Watson, *I Believe in Evangelism* (Hodder & Stoughton: London, 1975).

Footnotes

1 A discussion between George Peters and the Indian

evangelist Bakht Singh, *Evangelical Missions Tomorrow*, Wade Coggins, editor (William Carey Library: Pasadena, 1977) p 167.

2   William Carey, 'An Enquiry into the Obligation of Christians . . .' in Ralph Winter, *Perspectives on the World Christian Movement — a Reader* (William Carey Library: Pasadena, 1981) pp 227-237.

3   George Peters, *A Biblical Theology of Missions* (Moody Press: Chicago, 1972) p 173.

4   David Watson, *I Believe in Evangelism* (Hodder & Stoughton: London, 1976) pp 35-37.

5   Johannes Blauw, *The Missionary Nature of the Church* (Lutterworth Press: London, 1962) pp 110-111.

6   Peter T O'Brian, 'The Great Commission of Mt 28:18-20', *Evangelical Review of Theology* Vol 2, No 2 (1978) p 259.

16

THE POWER OF THE SPIRIT

In 1952, God spoke to Tommy Hicks through a vision and told him to go to South America and preach the Gospel. In 1954, while on his way to Buenos Aires, the name Peron flashed into his mind. He knew nobody by that name and near the flight's destination he asked the stewardess whether she knew anyone by that name. She replied that it was the name of the President. Hicks sought an appointment with Mr Peron but ran into difficulties. Then, an extraordinary event took place at the President's office. While seeking an interview, Hicks encountered Mr Peron's secretary, who had a bad leg. Hicks prayed for him and he was instantly healed. This resulted in Hicks being introduced to Mr Peron.

Peron received Hicks warmly and instructed his assistant to give Hicks whatever he asked for. On Hicks' request, a large stadium was made available to them as well as free access to the government-controlled radio and press. The campaign lasted for fifty-two days with Hicks preaching the Gospel on the saving power of Jesus with a strong emphasis on divine healing. Some 200,000 people attended the campaign on the final night. Almost all the churches grew as a result of the campaign. The Assemblies of God alone grew from 174 in 1951 to nearly 2,000 in 1956.[1]

'Missionary work as an expression of the Holy Spirit has received such slight and casual attention that it might almost escape the notice of a hasty reader . . . it is in the revelation of the Holy Spirit as a missionary Spirit that Acts stands alone in the New Testament.'[2]

It is frequently surprising how little is mentioned about

150

the ministry of the Holy Spirit with regard to the theology of mission. The Holy Spirit is certainly acknowledged as important, but his actual vital involvement is often ignored.

The most distinctive difference between the Old and New Testaments is in the one who baptises with the Holy Spirit. In the Old Testament men were endued with the power of God only on isolated occasions and for specific tasks. When Jesus was about to leave his disciples he promised to send a helper who would remain with them and in them: 'But I tell you the truth: It is for your good that I am going away. Unless I go away, the Counsellor will not come to you; but if I go, I will send him to you' (John 16:7).

The vital importance of the Holy Spirit is shown by the fact that the Great Commission is directly linked with his coming. Both in Luke 24:49 and Acts 1:8 the Commission is qualified by the need to wait until the Holy Spirit equips the disciples with power. It was at Pentecost that Christian mission truly began, and not with the giving of the Great Commission.

The Witnessing Spirit
During his time with the disciples at the last Passover feast, Jesus spoke much about the Holy Spirit: 'When the Counsellor comes, whom I will send to you from the Father, the Spirit of truth who goes out from the Father, he will testify about me, but you must also testify, for you have been with me from the beginning' (John 15:26, 27).

Pentecost
Luke first gives his description of the coming of the Spirit in Acts 2:1-7, and then he gives Peter's explanation. In his description, Luke speaks of three signs accompanying the coming of the Spirit: a sound — like a rushing wind; a sight — like fire; a speech — universally intelligible.

A crowd quickly gathered when people heard the noise. Luke makes a point of the cosmopolitan nature of the people (Acts 2:8-11) and their amazement at each one hearing the message in their own language. Pentecost was a dramatic reversal of the scattering which occurred at Babel.

151

Now these dispersed peoples were united in a new way by the Holy Spirit.

Peter clarified the situation by explaining that the phenomenon that people were witnessing was not a matter of intoxication, but a fulfilment of an ancient prophecy. The prophecy of Joel was a promise that in the last days God would pour out his Spirit on everyone (Acts 2:17). Here again we have the universal concern of God, both for the Jew and the Gentile.

The heart of Peter's message, and the focus of the Gospel message is Jesus. This is not the Jesus of myth or speculation, but the Jesus of history. In this first Gospel message of the new era Peter recounts the historical facts of the life of Jesus, underlining the Old Testament basis for His ministry and showing again that it is rooted in specific space and time.

In response to the message, the people were convicted and asked, 'Brothers, what shall we do?' (Acts 2:37). In turn Peter gave them two commands and two promises. First, they were to repent. This is a radical change of opinion concerning one's sin and about the person of Christ. Secondly, they were to be baptised in his name, the very name that they had initially denied. Then they would receive two free gifts from God: forgiveness of sin, and the Holy Spirit, who was not just for the apostles, nor for any particular group, but for all: 'The promise is for you and your children and for all who are far off — for all whom the Lord our God will call' (Acts 2:39). Some three thousand people responded that day.

The New Community

The most significant factor at Pentecost was that a new community came into being — the people of the Spirit. God had been active in one specific people, the Jews, but now the limits had been removed. To this cosmopolitan group Peter presents a universal appeal. The only restriction now lies in the need for repentance and faith in Christ. Christianity is not just for one's individual well-being, but to bring one into a new community — the Church.

Revival

The book of Acts illustrates the ministry of the Holy Spirit initiating new areas of missionary activity on several occasions. The four most notable examples each usher in a movement among a particular group.

Chapter	Place	People
2:3	Jerusalem	Jews
8:15-18	Samaria	Samaritans
10:44-45	Caesarea	Romans (Gentiles)
19:6	Ephesus	Asians (Gentiles)

Throughout the history of the Church, God has moved in outstanding ways during particular periods. These have been variously called 'revivals', or 'evangelical awakenings' but are all characterised by the power of the Spirit in a particular way. The term 'revival' has been widely used though often without clarity. Edwin Orr[3] has identified the term 'revival' for the particular work of God within the lives of the people of God which brings about an exhibition of New Testament Christianity. He would regard an 'awakening' as the work of God within the lives of non-Christians. Used in this way, the term 'revival' only applies to believers. However, the renewed vitality that these believers come to know in the Christian life becomes in itself a witness to neighbouring non-Christians. This in turn leads to the subsequent growth of the Church in a wider religious awakening.

The effects of such religious movements on individuals and nations are considerable, as described below:

'By 1739 it was beyond question that a great revival had commenced in England. New Year's Day witnessed the small group of leaders in London, including Whitefield and Wesley, met in a prayer meeting reminiscent of the private gatherings of ministers in the previous century. In the next five weeks Whitefield preached some 30 times in and about London; then moving to the Bristol area he took the momentous step on February 17th of preaching to

153

some 200 colliers in the open air at Kingswood, the use of a church having been denied to him. From this point onwards open-air preaching became an inescapable necessity as congregations gathered in thousands. In the bleak months of February and March Whitefield estimated that there were as many as 10,000 hearers on one occasion at Kingswood . . . . Physical side effects resulting from intense conviction of sin were to follow the evangelical revival throughout its course. Especially was this the case in the American colonies where the local revivals witnessed in a few places in the previous decade became, in 1740, 'the Great Awakening'. Everywhere the reign of formality seemed to have been broken and tears streamed down the faces of thousands under the preaching of the gospel.'[4]

Not only did many people become committed Christians, but they exerted a positive social and political influence. William Carey, the so-called father of modern missions, was influenced by this revival, and the evangelical wing of the Church of England, including the Keswick Convention, owes its origin to this movement.[4]

The Empowering Spirit

Jesus speaks of the Great Commission and the work in it of the Holy Spirit in terms of 'power' (Greek *dunamos* — the ability to do). In Luke 24:49 Jesus speaks about the 'power from on high', clearly relating this enabling to a divine supernatural source. This power works in the life of the new community, and it is with this power that the community will fulfil its mission. It is essential in any discussion on the empowering of the Holy Spirit, however, to recognise that the Holy Spirit is a person — in fact the third person of the Trinity. One must avoid thinking of the Spirit as 'parcels of power'. As with any person, his acquaintance must be cultivated.

Spiritual Conflict

On many occasions in the New Testament mission is spoken

of as a conflict between two opposing forces. In the Matthew account (12:22-31), Jesus makes it clear that the struggle in which he is engaged is not a civil war within a kingdom but a battle between the kingdom of God and the kingdom of Satan. Jesus gave to the disciples the mission to go out and preach the Kingdom. It was in their preaching and miracles that Jesus saw Satan fall (Luke 10:18).

This did not mean that the war was over. Jesus through his life and death was to gain the victory, but it would have to be claimed by his followers. Oscar Cullman[5] sought to illustrate this from World War II. D-Day was June 6th 1944, which proved to be the decisive turning point in the whole war. However, the war was not over at that time, and battle still continued until VJ-Day in 1945 Likewise Jesus established the victory, but it is not yet fully realised here on earth.

Miracles

The longer ending of the Mark account lays great emphasis upon the signs and wonders that would accompany the preaching of the Gospel. There has been much debate over the years as to the nature and possibility of miracles. Rev Jim Graham[6] has made a useful analysis of the nature of a miracle by saying that a miracle is three things at one time. First, it is a natural event occurring within the realm of nature. Secondly, it is an unnatural event in that it cuts across the normal laws of nature. Thirdly, it is a supernatural event in that it originates from outside the created order.

The continual reference to the Holy Spirit and the supernatural sphere is the key issue in miracles. If one's worldview does not accept the possibility of a supernatural deity who is able to influence directly space and time, then one cannot accept the concept of miracles. The secular Western worldview is basically materialistic in its assumptions, conceiving of a 'closed universe' in which nothing exists other than that which can be ordinarily sensed by man. These assumptions logically lead to the conclusion that miracles cannot happen. There must always be some logical, scientific answer. The Bible, however, does not assume such a 'closed universe', and so miracles are an accepted part of the activity of God in his world.

Whether one 'sees' a miracle depends upon whether or not one believes in the possibility of miracles. If one's worldview excludes such, then miracles would not be expected to occur. By way of illustration: a young man with a Christian party visiting Switzerland damaged his knee badly while skiing. The Swiss specialist confirmed that the X-ray photographs showed major damage and the need for surgery. Arrangements were made for him to fly home for the operation. As one of the leaders of the party I was asked to gather a group to pray for his healing. After prayer he felt that something had happened in his knee, but as the swelling was still pronounced it was felt that he should still return home. He was met at Heathrow airport and taken directly to a major London hospital. Once again X-ray photographs were taken, but this time there was no sign of damage. The Swiss specialist was known to the London doctors who highly respected his judgement. The doctors found it difficult to explain the difference between the two sets of X-ray photographs. The young man was therefore kept in hospital for a further two days before being discharged. He needed no operation.

Western man – especially Western scientific man – needs to ask himself whether his worldview – so effective in many areas of life – is without fault here. Most Eastern societies, on the other hand, quite readily accept the possibility of miracles, because their worldviews do not include the notion of a 'closed universe'.

Jesus told his disciples that miracles would confirm the preaching of the Gospel (John 14:12). Throughout the history of the Church there have been innumerable reports of miracles. However, miracles have never provided immediate evidence to the validity of the Gospel. The Pharisees refused to accept that Jesus had healed the blind man in John chapter 9, although they had no other explanation. When Jesus was tempted in the wilderness, he refused to perform the miraculous to establish his identity. The abuse

156

of the miraculous, as he knew, can lead to an excessive and dangerous triumphalism.

The Guiding Spirit
The Holy Spirit is not only the Spirit who gives power, He is also the one who reveals, leads, and speaks (John 16:13). He is the one who guides with respect to the nature and practice of mission. The book of Acts continually refers to the Holy Spirit guiding and leading with regard to the missionary work of the young Church.

First, the Spirit is the one who initiates new missionary ventures. This is most clearly seen in Acts 13:2-3: 'While they were worshipping the Lord and fasting, the Holy Spirit said, "Set apart for me Barnabas and Saul for the work to which I have called them".'

Secondly, on frequent occasions the Spirit guides different disciples, for example Philip (Acts 8:29), Peter (Acts 10:19), and Paul (Acts 16:6-9). On some occasions the Spirit is described as restraining the apostles (16:7), while on other occasions the apostles speak of having visions or dreams (10:9-17; 16:9-10). However, it is notable that the apostles did not solely rely on such supernatural directions in the fulfilment of their missions. The use of common sense to fulfil the purposes of God was clearly evident. The apostles knew the will of God as it was stated in the Great Commission and went out to do it. They were co-workers with God and recognised the responsibility and privilege which was theirs. (II Cor 5:20-6:2).

Thirdly, they were concerned not only with the message of the Gospel itself, but the reality of that message in their own lives: 'Therefore, since through God's mercy we have this ministry, we do not lose heart. Rather, we have renounced secret and shameful ways; we do not use deception, nor do we distort the Word of God. On the contrary, by setting forth the truth plainly we commend ourselves to every man's conscience in the sight of God' (II Cor 4:1, 2).

It is through the enabling power of the Holy Spirit that the mission of God will be accomplished, because the individual has been made new (Rom 12:1, 2). This new lifestyle will have an influence wider than just that covered by the redemption mandate. It will spread to the cultural mandate to make an integrated, consistent witness to the new life in Christ. It is the person of the Holy Spirit who makes the reality of the Kingdom feasible both in New Testament times and in this age.

Discussion Questions

1 Study how Paul was led by the Holy Spirit in Acts chapter 16. What lessons can be learned of the way God guides in present day situations?

2 Consider Ephesians 6:10-18. How does this apply to missionaries, pastors, and evangelists, and their ability to deal with situations on a 'supernatural level'?

3 Some people have argued that nothing but a visitation of the Holy Spirit can bring about a large-scale turning of people to Christ. Have we gone wrong when we have organised evangelistic campaigns rather than calling upon the Lord in prayer to send revival?

Recommended Reading

Michael Green, *I Believe in the Holy Spirit* (Hodder & Stoughton: London, 1970).

Michael Griffiths, *Serving Grace* (MARC Europe: London, 1986).

Frederick Dale Bruner, *A Theology of the Holy Spirit* (Hodder & Stoughton: London, 1970).

Harry R Boer, *Pentecost & Missions*, (Eerdmans Publishing Co: Grand Rapids, USA, 1961).

Colin Whittaker, *Great Revivals* (Marshalls: Basingstoke, 1984).

David Pytches, *Come Holy Spirit – Learning to Minister in Power* (Hodder & Stoughton: London, 1986).

Footnotes

1   Adapted from Peter Wagner, *Look Out! The Pentecos-*

tals Are Coming (Coverdale House Publishers: London, 1973), pp 19-22.

2   Rolland Allen, *Missionary Methods: St. Paul's Methods or Ours* (World Dominion: London, 1953).

3   Edwin J Orr, 'The Outpouring of the Spirit in Revival & Awakening and Its Issues in Church Growth' (Personal publication of Edwin Orr, 1984).

4   Iain H Murray, *the Puritan Hope* (Banner of Truth Trust: Edinburgh, 1971) pp 115-6.

5   Oscar Cullmann, *Christ & Time* (SCM Press: London, 1951).

6   Jim Graham, Private Comment to the Author.

7   C S Lewis *Miracles* (Geoffrey Bles: London, 1947).

17

THE COMMUNITY OF THE KINGDOM

It was a typical hot, sticky day as I walked to the church in a large Indian city. As I turned the corner, I heard the first sounds of the organ playing one of Wesley's famous hymns. The church was set in its own walled grounds, with a pleasant line of trees leading to the church door. The stone building resembled a typical English church, apart from the fact that the windows were wide open and fans were leisurely wafting draughts of air on the assembled company. The men wore white shirts and some even had ties, and they sat with their families on pews looking towards the pulpit at the front.

As I joined the congregation, the minister, wearing a clerical collar entered and announced the first hymn. We all stood to sing, 'O for a thousand tongues to sing . . .' and soon we were under way in the service which was a model of that found in many parts of the United Kingdom.

The previous Sunday, I had attended a rather different church in the same town. Here, we had left our shoes at the door as we entered a rectangular, well-ventilated building which was not immediately recognisable as a church. Inside, there were no chairs, only clean rush mats with a centre carpet leading to the front. I went to join the men who sat on the right, while my wife sat with the women and children on the left.

There was no organ here, only the drums, flutes and stringed instruments characteristic of this part of India. The people were singing in their own language a psalm that had been translated and adapted to an Indian melody. The service continued for about four hours with a sermon lasting one and a half hours, and a Communion service with its own distinctive character.[1]

The most important outcome of Pentecost was the formation of a new community, a people of the Spirit. God brought into being a people through whom he would show forth his character and his very life. As Melvin Hodges has said: 'The Church is God's agent in the earth — the medium through which he expresses himself to the world. God has no other redeeming agency in the earth.'[2] It would be through this people that God would continue to fulfil his mission.

Paradigms of the Church

One of our major difficulties in understanding the biblical notion of the Church relates to the various mental models, or paradigms, that we have concerning the Church. The world 'church' conjures up many pictures which are often far from biblical in their concept. In English, the word 'church' has a wide range of meanings. Before considering the scriptural basis, it is worthwhile considering some of the various paradigms that the word 'church' brings to one's mind.

Some consider the Church as an institution. The emphasis of this view is upon the outward structures of organisation, government and buildings. While such elements are needed within every human institution, they are not what characterises the Church. The Greek word *ekklesia* which is translated by the word 'church' in the Authorised Version English Bible of 1611 was earlier translated by Tyndale as 'congregation'. Tyndale's translation rightly placed the emphasis upon the people rather than on the organisation of the people.

Others consider the Church to be a mystical, or otherworldly reality. As a spiritual reality the Church is seen as some perfect, ethereal reality comprising all true believers. The Church is indeed a spiritual reality, but it is also in existence here on the earth.

Yet others, primarily Reformers, defined the Church as being the people of God. These people, and the congregations they formed, could be recognised by three distinct

161

marks. Initially, there was preaching which emphasised the exposition of the Word of God. Then there were the sacraments, restricted to the two ordained by Christ — baptism and the Lord's Supper. Finally, there was church discipline which maintained the standards of the Scriptures in the everyday life of the members.

A fourth view which has emerged during the last few years may be called the 'charismatic view'. Emphasis has again been placed on the concept of the Church as the people of God, but this is revealed by a unity based on a common experience of the Holy Spirit, and not necessarily on theological or denominational position.

The difficulty with each of these four definitions is that they fail to take into account the cultural dimension as well as the biblical principles. One's view of the nature of the Church is of vital importance in cross-cultural missionary work, and should be able to distinguish clearly the theological principles from the cultural expression. To achieve a full understanding of the concept of 'Church', we must approach the topic from both theological and sociological perspectives.

Theological Principles

The word *ekklesia* in its first-century secular usage meant a meeting or gathering of people. This word was used in the translation of the Septuagint to describe the assembly of the people of Israel, especially when they were summoned by Yahweh (Deut 4:10; 18:16). Stephen uses the word when speaking of the people of Israel assembled in the desert (Acts 7:38). The continuation of the Old Testament concept of the people of God into that of the Church is clearly apparent.

This connection is further emphasised in I Peter 2:9-10: 'But you are a chosen people, a royal priesthood, a holy nation, a people belonging to God, that you may declare the praises of him who called you out of darkness into his wonderful light.' These four descriptions are all borrowed from the Old Testament, and are clearly intended to portray that the Church is thus involved in the mission of Israel.[3]

A Chosen Race

This expression has been borrowed from Isaiah 43:20. The word 'race' is the translation of the Greek word *genos* in which the emphasis is placed upon the origin of the people. The origin of this people is a result of an election from out of the world. As the word *ekklesia* itself reveals, they are called out of the world in order to proclaim the great acts of God in the world.

A Royal Priesthood

The Old Testament usage of priest, as in Exodus 19:5-6, places the emphasis upon the mediatoral role in which the priest stands before God on behalf of the people. The distinction between priest and laity is put away and the whole church is here portrayed as a priesthood. As such their worship and praise itself can bear witness to him. Because one is partaking in this kind of priestly service to the King, it becomes a royal service.

A Holy Nation

In the Old Testament, out of all the nations, only the people of Israel are called holy. In I Peter 2:9-10, the Greek word chosen is *ethnos* which is the word usually used for the peoples of the world as opposed to the Jews themselves. This usage must therefore be an indication that the community of the Church has taken over the place of Israel. The Gentiles who were unholy in themselves have been sanctified by coming to Christ. They are now separated for God, and so are God's people.

God's Possession

The Greek word *peripoiesin* suggests a dynamic intervention of God himself to acquire and keep his people—*laos*. As we have seen, this emphasis upon a people of God is one of the great themes throughout Scripture. In Exodus 6:7 God declares: 'I will take you as my own people, and I will be your God.' At the end of the book of Revelation, in the description of the holy city, one finds the same reference, 'They will be his people' (Rev 21:2, 3).

These texts leave one in no doubt that the people of God are called for service to the world. That service is to declare the 'wonderful acts of God'. Here the Church is revealed as 'a light for the Gentiles' (Isa 42:5, 6). God's missionary programme now continues with and through his people, the Church. In Christ a new creation has arisen, the community of the Kingdom.

As J H Yoder has said, 'The political novelty which God brings into the world is a community of those who serve instead of ruling; who suffer instead of inflicting suffering; whose fellowship crosses social lines instead of reinforcing them. This new community . . . is not only a vehicle of the Gospel or fruit of the Gospel; it is the Good News.'[4]

Sociological Principles

Within the New Testament the word *ekklesia* is used to describe two main concepts. First is the idea of the universal Church which encompasses the worldwide community of Christian people, both living and dead. This is what is meant by the Nicene Creed when it speaks of 'one Catholick, Apostolic Church'.

The second meaning relates to the local community of Christians meeting within a specific geographical region. Paul uses the word in this sense when he writes to the churches of Galatia or Macedonia. As such the local church is a sociological entity with a visible presence within the community. It is important to emphasise that the local church is not just a part of the universal Church, but is the local expression of the Church. All the resources of Christ are available to every local congregation.

Church Structures

Although the universal Church is not an institution, the Church must have distinct sociological structures in its local expression. The people of God will organise their activities, even their religious activities, along certain patterns. It is foolish to think that one can avoid such structures because man is by his very nature a social being. As Moberg has said, 'Every religious organisation has some degree of formalism or institutionalisation. This is true of groups that claim to be "merely a fellowship, not a denomination", and of those so informally and loosely organised that they claim to lack organisation altogether.'[5]

Snyder has made a useful distinction between those issues of the Church which are sociological, and those which are of theological and eternal importance. He has called the two 'para-church' and 'church' respectively.[6] Unfortunately, the term 'para-church' is often used in a variety of ways different from that understood by Snyder. This has lead to some confusion, and for this reason we will use the term 'sociological structures' rather than 'para-church'. The following chart illustrates the important distinctions that he is trying to make.

Differences Between the universal Principles of the Church and the Sociological Structures

UNIVERSAL PRINCIPLES	SOCIOLOGICAL STRUCTURES
1 God's creation	1 Man's creation
2 Spiritual fact	2 Sociological fact
3 Cross-culturally valid	3 Culturally bound
4 Biblically understood & evaluated	4 Sociologically understood & evaluated
5 Validity determined by spiritual qualities & fidelity to Scripture	5 Validity determined by function in relation to the mission of the Church
6 God's agent of evangelism and reconciliation	6 Man's agent for evangelism and service
7 Essential	7 Expendable
8 Eternal	8 Temporal & temporary
9 Divine revelation	9 Human tradition
10 Purpose to glorify God	10 Purpose to serve the Church

Snyder's list tends to simplify the close relationship which exists between these two aspects, but it does highlight certain features which are essential in understanding the missionary task of the Church and the way it should be achieved. It is all too easy for any local church to confuse the important spiritual issues of the Church with the sociological structures, and in so doing make the structures themselves sacred. These structures are then communicated as equally important to the principles of the Church.

This is best understood by way of an illustration. The Bible encourages believers to meet together for worship, but it gives little guidance as to exactly how the meeting will be conducted. In Britain for many years the general pattern of Sunday worship has consisted of the singing of four or five hymns, interspersed by prayers, Bible reading, collection, and a sermon. Why do we follow this pattern? Why do we choose to sing hymns to the music of an organ? The primary reason is that these particular social structures have become the accepted patterns of church worship. There is nothing wrong with having such patterns, but we must realise that these structures are not part of the universal principles of the Church. They may be changed without altering the very nature of the Church.

The Indigenous Church

Just as a great river is fed by many streams and divides into many distributaries, so the 'river' of God's people finds its own sociological structures to enable worship of God in spirit and truth — a worship that varies in expression. Here Snyder's thesis provides some useful guidelines. It first allows one to see the Church as being both relevant to a particular culture and yet at the same time not culturally bound. Secondly, it allows one to modify church structure without distorting the very biblical nature of the Church. Finally, it makes it possible for one to appreciate a wide variety of church structures, which Snyder calls 'biblical legitimacy'.

This understanding is of vital importance for the cross-cultural ministry of the Church. It means that although the basic spiritual nature of the Church remains unchanged throughout all societies, the various structures expressing that nature may, and probably will, change.

During the 1950's this concept was spoken of as 'the indigenous church'. The term borrowed from horticulture was applied to the national church which 'shares the life of the country in which it is planted and finds within itself the ability to govern itself, support itself, and reproduce itself.'[7] Meanwhile Smalley has defined an indigenous church in the following way: 'It is a group of believers who live out their life, including their socialised Christian activity, in the patterns of the local society, and for whom any transformation of that society comes out of their felt needs under the guidance of the Holy Spirit and the Scriptures.'[8] This definition recognises some important principles:

1 The local church is a society within, and formed out of, the multicultural nature of humankind. Israel as the people of God was essentially a mono-cultural community, but now the Church is a multi-cultural community. The local church will indeed reflect the multi-cultural character.

2 The sociological patterns (Snyder's 'para-church') of a particular local church will be based upon those patterns already existing within the local society. For example, Christians may choose to use their traditional musical instruments for worship rather than foreign instruments such as an organ. Their church buildings, too, may be constructed along traditional local patterns.

3 The local sociological patterns will be transformed by the Holy Spirit, both in the lives of the individual believers and within the church as a whole. This transformation will produce a common characteristic among all local churches as the life of Christ is made real and relevant among them.

One finds a tension here between the unity and the diversity of the Christian Church. The oneness of the Church is continually stressed in the New Testament, but that does not mean that uniformity should dominate the people of God. Within our multi-cultural world the issue of the Church and culture is one of growing importance, to which we will return in greater detail in chapter 19.

Discussion Questions

1 In what does the 'unity' of the Church consist, and how should it be expressed? What is the relationship between 'uniformity' and 'unity'?

2 Give a list of the descriptions of the Church in the New Testament. What were the purposes of God in bringing the Church into being?

3 Consider the patterns of worship within your own church. Can you distinguish between the universal principles and the sociological structures?

Recommended Reading

Howard A Snyder, *New Wineskins* (Marshall, Morgan & Scott: London, 1976).

Howard A Snyder, *The Community of the King* (IVP: Illinois, 1978).

Melvin Hodges, *On the Mission Field: The Indigenous Church* (Moody Press: Chicago, 1953).

Footnotes

1 Excerpt from Monica Hill, *How To Plant Churches* (MARC Europe: London, 1984) p 45.

2 Melvin Hodges, *A Guide to Church Planting* (Moody Press: Chicago, 1973) p 15.

3 J Blauw, *The Missionary Nature of the Church* (Lutterworth Press: London, 1962) p 126.

4 John Howard Yoder, *The Politics of Jesus* (Eerdmans: Grand Rapids, 1972) p 192.

5 David O Moberg, *The Church as a Social Institution* (Prentice-Hall: London, 1962) pp 118-124.

6 Howard A Snyder, *New Wineskins* (Marshall, Morgan & Scott: London, 1976) pp 147-156 and p 162.

7 Melvin Hodges, *On the Mission Field* (Moody Press: Chicago, 1953), p 7.

8 W A Smalley, 'Cultural Implications of the Indigenous Church', in C Kraft, & T N Whisley, *Readings in Dynamic Indigeneity* (William Carey Library: Pasadena, 1979) p 35.

18

THE GROWTH OF
THE CHURCH

Out of the thousands turning to Christ, only eight Danis were baptised at Kelila on Sunday, July 29th, 1962. Four thousand crowded around the pool, among them a group from Bokondini, their former enemies. No spears. No arrows. Here and there grease, soot, and feathers of those who had come not yet to participate . . . Each man and woman was quiet, expectant, reverent.

A little man, Jawon, the first of the candidates, came forward.

'I used to be in great darkness and did many sins. Then I heard the Word of God, and how the Son of God gave His life for me. I believe the Word of God and I am His child. I now confess openly before you all that I am identified with the Lord who died for me and rose again.'

The missionary reached out and took his hand.

'Jawon do you believe that Jesus Christ is the Son of God?'

'Epe aret (that is true).'

Then Jawon, the first Kelila Dani, went down into the waters of baptism.

One after another, five men and a married couple followed Jawon.

Monthly a steady number was added to the first eight.

At Pentecost, the new community of the Kingdom came into being, and almost immediately it began to grow. Through the preaching of Peter the church grew from about 120 to over 3,000 in a single day. Throughout the book of Acts the growth of this new community continued. The aspect of the growth of the Church has been re-emphasised

169

in recent years by the teaching of Donald McGavran,[2] who has highlighted the need for an appreciation of the Church as something not static, but dynamic and progressive in the purposes of God.

The Growth Concept

Jesus came teaching about the kingdom of God, and a major aspect of that teaching is that the Kingdom will grow. The agricultural motif of so many of the Kingdom parables, such as that of the mustard seed and the yeast, leaves one in no doubt about the growth of the Kingdom. However, Jesus made it equally clear that growth would not come about without opposition. The parable of the weeds (Matt 13:24-30, 36-43) reveals the existence of an enemy who will try to pollute and confuse the harvest.

In sending out his disciples, Jesus clearly demonstrated his concern to bring in the 'lost sheep of the house of Israel' (Matt 10). The Great Commission likewise reveals that the desire of the King is that his Kingdom should increase, and his words show this intention: 'I will build my church' (Matt 16:18). Growth is therefore an integral part of the Kingdom and also of the Church.

The question for discussion is not whether the Church should grow, but in what ways growth occurs and by what means. Various models have been put forward to examine the growth of the Church, but as with all models they have their limitations. Any organisation can be described by two sets of factors: first, the particular people attached to the group, and secondly, the degree of commitment to the aims of the group. Traditionally in church growth thinking this has been called 'quantitative' and 'qualitative' growth. These two aspects to growth may be considered under the headings of evangelism and Body-life.

Evangelism

The evangelistic mandate given by Christ to his disciples was irrepressibly fulfilled after Pentecost. The telling of the Good News of the Kingdom was considered the first priority of the Church's ministry. The Greek word *euangelizo-*

mai means the proclamation of the *euangelion* or Good News. It is almost exclusively used in the New Testament for the sharing of the Good News that the kingdom of God has broken into lives of men through the person of Jesus Christ, the King. Men are called to respond to this message in repentance and faith.

Peter Wagner[3] has popularised the concept of '3-P' evangelism, by which he means 'presence, proclamation and persuasion'. By 'presence' he means the Christian life being lived out in the midst of a people, the so-called 'silent witness' of doing good. It is from this context that proclamation should occur. In addition to proclamation, he would add the element of persuasion, in which the evangelist seeks to reveal the fundamental importance of the message to the individual, but this must in no way be confused with coercion. The Christian responsibility is to communicate faithfully the message with the hope that people will respond, but the results are ultimately with the Sovereign God.

The parable of the sower (Matt 13:3-23) illustrates that people differ in their responsiveness to the 'seed'. Just because one group does not respond to the *euangelion*, it does not mean that evangelism has not occurred. To evangelise in its biblical usage does not mean to win converts, but to announce the Good News.[4] However, the sower goes forth sowing with the intention that a harvest will result.

Body Growth

The growth of the Church must not be seen merely as an increase in the number of members, but as a development of the Kingdom within it, both for the individual and corporately. Acts 2:42-47 reveals how the young Church began to grow as a spiritual community. This was as a result of its learning from the apostles. The apostles' instruction was derived in turn from Christ, who had instructed them, and now Christ was authenticating their ministry by miracles. The teaching of the apostles is found in the New Testament writings; the study of and meditation on these Scriptures should therefore not be neglected by any Christian community today.

Church growth also resulted from the community's fellowship (*koinonia*). Here in Acts 2:42 is the first use of this word which introduces a new depth of relationship in this Christian community. This multi-cultural, spirit-filled community entered into a relationship that showed itself in practical caring for the needs of one another. The Christians were concerned about the social needs of others and shared their money and property as they were able, and as there was need.

Worship, too, was an essential key to the growth of the body. Prayer and praise were fundamental parts of the Early Church and should be a spontaneous response of the people of God to their Lord.

Church Ministries

An important aspect of the growth of the Church is the exercise of spiritual gifts. Many books have in recent years been written on the subject of spiritual gifts,[5] and it seems necessary here only to refer to those which particularly relate to the mission of the Church. Along this line the gifts may be classified into three main groups:

First, there is ability to communicate. Several of the gifts particularly relate to the verbal expression of spiritual truths — the word of wisdom, the word of knowledge, prophecy, teaching, exhortation, speaking in tongues, and even the ministry of the apostle and evangelist are those of communication of the Gospel. Secondly are the gifts of demonstration: healings, miracles, faith, and discernment of spirits. Thirdly, there are those gifts for the administration and organisation of the local church, i.e. service, giving and administration.

All the spiritual gifts are relevant for mission in one way or another. The growth of the Christian community occurs through the exercise of these gifts, which cause the Church to be built up as the people of God (Eph 4:12). As such, the Church will be a witness amongst the nations, and will fulfil the promise given to Abraham that he will be a blessing to all nations. In this way all Christians can be witnesses, irrespective of their particular gifts.

However, there are those gifts which may especially enable the Christian to share his faith with others. The evangelist would be an obvious case. The role of the missionary may be a little more complex, depending upon how one defines a missionary. One frequently hears the statement, 'Every Christian is a missionary!' In the context of spiritual gifts this is not the case, and probably what is meant is 'Every Christian is a witness!' The term 'missionary' may most usefully be attributed to those attempting to share their faith with people of other cultures. Their work will entail their learning another language, adapting to another way of life, and properly communicating their faith with others.

Mission Structures

Although the missionary task of the Church must begin and emanate from the local church, a major feature of the modern missionary movement has been the emergence and growth of specific mission organisations. In recent years these organisations have been challenged as to their biblical basis. Are missionary societies in fact biblical, or are they usurping the role of the local church?

If one looks at the New Testament for explicit patterns for missionary agencies one would be disappointed. There is no express pattern for such agencies in just the same way as one would not find a specific blueprint for Sunday schools, Bible Schools, or many of the other organisations which characterise today's Church. The answer to the confusion lies in one distinction Snyder[6] makes between church and sociological structures ('para-Church')[7]. Although the Church has eternal principles which are unchanging, the social structures will change. The Church must always assess these structures in the light of the eternal principles.

Acts 13

Although mission was undertaken by the young church from the time of Pentecost, the record of Acts 13 reveals that something new came into being. 'In the church at Antioch there were prophets and teachers. . . . While they were worshipping the Lord and fasting, the Holy Spirit said, "Set apart for me Barnabas and Saul, for the work to which I have called them" ' (Acts 13:1, 2).

Several points arise from this passage. First, the initiative for this new activity came not from the Church, but from the Holy Spirit, although it may well have been related to the fact of their prayer and fasting. Secondly, those called were functioning members of the local church, and part of the Church universal; they continued to remain part of the Church universal. Thirdly, the 'call' of the Holy Spirit was recognised by the local church, and acted upon.

What came into being at this time, then, was a new sociological structure. It came into being not to compete with the local church structure, but to supplement it in the fulfilling of its mission. Both are local expressions of the Church Universal.[8]

The Apostolic Band

This new structure had various characteristics that are worth examination. Note first that the group sent out by the church at Antioch was a mobile team, unlike the local church from which they went, which was geographically defined. The mobility of this new structure enabled the mission of the Church to advance much more rapidly through the world.

There was also a flexibility within the team. Paul's team involved members from several local churches during his ministry.

Barnabas & John Mark	Antioch (13:3)
Silas	Jerusalem (15:22)
Timothy	Lystra (16:3)
Luke	Troas (16:8-11)
Erastus	Ephesus (19:22)
Gaius	Derbe (19:29 & 20:4)
Sopater	Beroea (20:4)
Aristarchus & Secundus	Thessalonica (20:4)

The team's leadership was distinct from that of any local

174

church. Although the church at Antioch initially sent Paul and Barnabas out, and the missionaries did return and report back to the church, it is important to realise that they were not under the direction of the local church. The itinerant nature of their work necessitated their being free to obey the dictates of the Holy Spirit within a particular situation.

Paul in a number of his letters strongly asserts his apostolic authority over the churches he had founded. This is especially seen in Galatians where Paul does so because the Gospel that he had brought was being undermined by the teaching of others. As Michael Griffiths has written: 'What was the nature of the missionaries' authority? We have seen that the apostle's authority as a teacher was the plain authority of the Word of God itself. It was the authority of the preacher and teacher to whom had been committed a message that he must deliver in full, neither more nor less.'[9]

Little is said, however, about the practical support of this missionary organisation. Nothing is reported of Paul receiving money from the church in Antioch, and only the church at Philippi is known to have sent him assistance (Phil 4:15).

Sodalities

Ralph Winter[10] has suggested that these two structures of local church and mission group have their origin within the Jewish society of that day. As we have already seen, the synagogue had become the centre of Jewish social and religious life, especially for the Jews of the diaspora. The local church came to incorporate many of the features of the synagogue. A second religious structure was that of the Pharasaic proselytisers who worked as small mobile bands and travelled around much of the Roman Empire. It would have been surprising had Paul not known of their activity and operation, and so these could have become the model, whether consciously or unconsciously, of his own band.

Ralph Winter also argues forcibly that down through the history of the Church these two structures can be distinctly observed. He has suggested calling them 'modality', which

175

refers to a wider society, and 'sodality', a more specific community within that modality. The monastries and Roman Catholic orders are examples of sodalities, as would be the modern missionary society. The Church in general is a modality.

One must be careful not to use the precedent of Paul's mission band as a biblical foundation for the modern Western highly organised mission agency. One may, however, argue that within the Early Church there existed agencies of mission which have their twentieth-century equivalent in the mission society. The structure and usefulness of these societies must come under the examination of the Church with regard to their nature and value — as must all sociological structures.

Sodalities, by their very nature, are activist organisations and provide means by which particular members of a church may fulfil specific tasks. The mission society has shown itself effective in enabling the Church to reach across cultures in its evangelistic mission. It allows specially trained and equipped people to live and work within other cultures, and so to fulfil the Great Commission. This requires them to be especially aware of the need for flexibility in new patterns of operation required by the changing world, and such awareness is the primary value of the modern missionary organisation.

Discussion Questions

1 Draw a design for your ideal church building. What assumptions about the life and function of the church are shown in the design?

2 Consider the particular characteristics of the apostle Paul which made him an effective missionary. What gifts, natural and spiritual, would you look for in a missionary recruit?

3 What can missionary societies do that the local churches would find difficult in fulfilling the Great Commission?

Recommended Reading

Peter C Wagner, *Your Spiritual Gifts Can Help Your Church Grow* (MARC Europe: London, 1985).

Michael Griffiths, *Serving Grace* (MARC Europe: London, 1986).

Ralph Winter, 'The Two Structures of God's Redemptive Mission' *Missiology* (Jan 1974, Vol II, No 1) pp 121-139.

Eddie Gibbs, *I Believe in Church Growth* (Hodder: London, 1981).

Michael Harper, *Let My People Grow* (Hodder: London, 1977).

Footnotes

1 Shirley Horne, *An Hour to the Stone Age* (Moody Press: Chicago, 1973) pp 160-161.

2 Donald McGavran, *Understanding Church Growth* (Eerdmans: Grand Rapids, 1970).

3 Peter Wagner, *Frontiers in Missionary Strategy* (Moody Press: Chicago, 1971).

4 John Stott, *Mission and the Modern World* (Falcon: London, 1975) p 38.

5 See Donald Bridge, & David Phyphers, *Spiritual Gifts & the Church* (IVP: Leicester, 1973) and Peter Wagner, *Your Spiritual Gifts Can Help Your Church Grow* (MARC Europe: London, 1985).

6 Howard Snyder, *The Community of the King* (IVP: Illinois, 1978) pp 160-162.

7 NB The term 'para-church' is used in various ways by different authors. One may identify at least three usages. First that of Snyder, described in this text. Secondly, an organisation outside the direct authority of the local church such as a missionary society. Thirdly, any organisation outside the authority of the established ecclesiastical denominations, e.g. a house church.

8 A W Swamidoss, 'The Biblical Basis of the Para-Church Movements' *Evangelical Review of Theology*, Vol 7, No 2 (1983) pp 192-206.

9 Michael Griffiths, 'Today's Missionaries, Yesterday's

Apostles', *Evangelical Missions Quarterly* Vol 21, No 2 (1983) p 160.

10   Ralph Winter, 'The Two Structures of God's Redemptive Mission', *Missiology* Vol 2, No 1 (1974) pp 121-139.

19

THE MULTI-CULTURAL PEOPLE OF GOD

When in Rome

While working in Rome this past summer, I found myself in a very interesting dilemma. In the Italian culture, wine is normally served with the meal as a predinner 'icebreaker' to guests one wishes to welcome courteously. The Italian does not associate use or non-use of wine with Christian behaviour as does the North American evangelical, who often uses it as a criterion for measuring the spirituality of a person.

I personally have no qualms about having wine with my meal while living in another culture that accepts this social norm, especially when I am a guest in the home of an Italian . . . .

One evening I was invited to dinner at the home of a friend named Carlo. Carlo was not a Christian and I had been introduced to him by his close friend Mario who was a Christian. Mario had been sharing his faith with Carlo for over a year.

To complicate the situation, Mr Long, an American evangelical missionary, had also been invited. He was trained in the same Christian college in which I was serving as a Dean of Students. He totally abstained from drinking wine, feeling it is unbecoming of a Christian. He had been serving in Italy for three years and though I had met him previously, I knew very little else about him and his missionary organisation.

Just about the time I was ready to ask Mr Long some questions about his background, Carlo walked into the room with a

tray of four glasses of wine. He served me first and I accepted.
Then he served Mario and proceeded to Mr Long. Mr Long
graciously refused.

So there I stood with my glass of wine. I didn't want to offend
Carlo after having accepted the wine. Neither did I want to
offend the missionary who totally abstained. Mr Long, I was
quite sure, knew I was Dean of Students at the college, further
complicating the decision I had to make. This was no time for a
letter to be sent to the college and to the board of trustees.

What should I do? . . . .[1]

This is a useful place to review the issues relating to the
multi-cultural nature of human society, and how these express themselves within the life of the Church today. In
chapter 4 we observed how, as a result of man's sin, God in
an act of judgement had confused the languages of man, and
in so doing had made humankind multi-cultural.

From the call of Abraham, God began to work in a special
and unique way within a single people — the Israelites. It
was through their particular religion and culture that God
was seeking to reveal himself to humankind. Although the
purposes of God were universal, people could only enter
into that salvation covenant by identifying with the people
and culture of Israel.

With the coming of Christ, this situation was totally
changed. Now a doorway was opened for all peoples to enter
into the salvation covenant in Christ. But how were the
Gentiles to enter into this new community? Did it mean that
they had to take on the culture of Israel as in the old
covenant? How could the Church, as the people of God, be
a multi-cultural community? These were the questions
which quickly came to the fore within the Early Church. An
examination of how these questions are dealt with in scripture gives revealing insight into how these same matters can
be considered with regard to present day cross-cultural
witness.

The Council of Jerusalem
The word 'culture' is not found in the Scriptures, but the

general questions relating to the way of life of the people are seen on numerous occasions in the book of Acts. The narrative of Peter and Cornelius illustrates the attitude of the Jews to the Gentiles with regard to their social relationship (Acts 10). A Jew would neither give or receive hospitality from a Gentile. However, in his dream Peter had been rebuked for considering as unclean anything that God had declared clean. Thus, when the servants of Cornelius came to Peter he invited them in, and later when he reached the home of Cornelius he surprised everyone by entering the house.

The issue of the relationship between Jewish and Gentile cultures, especially as it relates to the Church, was to come to a climax with the meeting at Jerusalem in Acts chapter 15, which has proved to be the most important missionary conference in the history of the Church.

The Problem

'Some men came down from Judaea to Antioch and were teaching the brothers: "Unless you are circumcised, according to the custom taught by Moses, you cannot be saved." This brought Paul and Barnabas into sharp dispute and debate with them . . . .' (Acts 15:1, 2). These men, who were to become known as the Judaisers, believed that Jesus was the Messiah, and salvation was to be found in him. But, they also believed that a man must be circumcised according to the old covenant. Most theologians have considered this issue only from the point of view of its religious significance, and although this is valuable, there is a wider issue involved.

It has already been stated that it was inconceivable to any Hebrew for a Gentile to enter into the salvation covenant with God without taking upon himself the whole of the Hebrew culture, and most significantly, the sign of circumcision.

The Word of God had become manifest within the Jewish culture, but now as the wider mission of the Church became significant, the question was, 'Does a Gentile have to take on Jewish culture if he is to become a Christian?' In a parallel consideration of today's situation one may ask, 'Does Christian conversion mean cultural conversion?' For example, when an African becomes a Christian, does he need to be encouraged to leave his traditional culture?

The Jews could rightly claim that God had been particularly active within their people and culture, making them a special people. The Exodus was a mighty demonstration of God acting on their behalf, revealing his power and his grace. The giving of the Law was the foundation of their way of life. What other nation could claim such a direct intervention from God? The Hebrew culture was not just a product of their environment, but a result of the involvement of the supra-cultural in their history (see figure 4:1). No wonder the Judaisers, in wanting the best for these new Gentile converts, wanted to see them circumcised and following the Jewish culture.

It is important that the cross-cultural missionary of any century realises the feelings of these first-century Judaisers. These men were Christians, and I believe concerned about the life of these new Gentile converts. However, they failed to perceive the fullness of what God was doing. The Jews considered Gentile cultures to be hopelessly corrupt and could see no way that a person as a Christian could remain in that culture. This brings us to vital questions in our approach with the Gospel to other cultures. Do we expect our converts to enter into our culture, or can they live as Christians in their own culture? Does today's Western missionary not have something of the same attitude when he looks at the 'pagan' societies of the world?

Discussion at the Council of Jerusalem — Acts 15

There are three main contributions to the debate. First, Peter acknowledges the sovereignty of God in this matter (verses 7-9). The events with Cornelius were clearly uppermost in Peter's mind, where God had taken the initiative. If God had given the Holy Spirit to Gentiles then it seems that God is not so concerned about outward aspects of culture when it comes to salvation. Salvation is through faith in Christ and does not depend upon the culture of a person.

Second to report are Barnabas and Paul, and they speak of 'all the miraculous signs and wonders God had done among the Gentiles through them' (verse 12). Through these signs, God is authenticating his concern for the Gentile peoples of the world.

Thirdly, it is James who, probably as chairman of the meeting, sums up much of what has been said: 'Simon has described to us how God at first showed his concern by taking from the Gentiles a people for himself' (verse 14). The meeting recognises that God is now at work among the Gentiles in the same way as he had been at work among the Jews in forming his Church. James stated that this is just what God had promised in Amos 9:11-12.[2] When the Kingdom of God comes into the world then the universal purposes of God will be fulfilled: 'that the remnant of men may seek the Lord and all the Gentiles who bear my name' (verse 17).

Two important recommendations result from the conference. First, a person need not be circumcised in order to become a Christian. In rejecting circumcision for Gentile converts the meeting also rejected cultural conversion. The decision underlined the conclusion that Christianity was not a sect of Judaism, but was distinctly multi-cultural and universal. The implications of this are immense for the Church as a whole.

With reference to the second recommendation, the council did, however, realise the need for some guidance in order that Christians would not be isolated from each other because of their different cultural practices. A major question of immediate importance was posed to the church. How could an orthodox Jew, though he has become a Christian, have social relations with a Gentile even if he too is a Christian? Certain basic social rules were therefore proposed:

1 The first rule concerned eating meat that had been offered to idols. Within the religious practices of the Mediterranean it was common for sacrifices to be made in the temples. The sacrificer would take most of the meat and make a feast for his friends, often in the temple grounds but

183

sometimes in his own home. The remaining part of the meat was given to the temple and sold for ordinary purpose. All such meat had therefore been offered to the gods and was ritually unclean. The Gentile Christians were instructed to refrain from eating this kind of meat.

2 Sexual immorality was common within the Graeco-Roman world and must clearly be avoided by all Christians.

3 The Gentile converts must also refrain from eating meat which had been killed by strangling. For the Greeks, such meat was a delicacy, but for the Jews the blood was the life. The Jews argued that as the blood flowed out, the life ebbed away also. All Jewish meat was killed and the blood drained off because the life belonged to God. The Gentile was therefore required to eat only meat prepared in the Jewish way, and in so doing, this would allow Jew and Gentile Christians to eat together.

Had these regulations not been observed no social relationships could have been established between the Jews and Gentiles of the Church. The Unity of the Church is of paramount importance, and members of the Church need to accommodate cultural issues in order to establish such unity. In spite of the fact that Luke in Acts now dismisses the issue, the epistles are a sufficient indication that the controversy was not settled as far as the extremists were concerned.

The Galatians Debate

The continuation of the problem of culture occurs in a number of Paul's letters, and especially in Galatians, Romans and Corinthians. It is in Galatians that Paul expressed the issues in their fullest form. Once again theologians have rightly dealt at length with this subject, but they have frequently limited their considerations to the religious aspects. In actual fact, the issues raised spread much further than the issue of circumcision to that of the whole Jewish Law, and finally to the whole Jewish culture.

Paul Rebukes Peter

Part of the life of the Early Church was the *agapé* feast (love feast), in which the whole community came together to enjoy a meal provided by pooling whatever resources they had. For a strict Jew it was forbidden to eat or go on a journey with a Gentile. Neither was it acceptable to give nor to accept hospitality from a Gentile, nor even to do business with one.

Peter at first forgot such taboos in the joy of the new fellowship, and shared a meal with Jew and Gentile alike. However, when certain Jewish Christians arrived, Peter withdrew from the common meal. It was then that Paul spoke with all the zeal of his passionate nature (Gal 2:11-21). He condemned Peter's hypocrisy with regard to eating with Gentiles: 'You are a Jew, yet you live like a Gentile and not like a Jew. How is it, then, that you force Gentiles to follow Jewish customs?' (verse 14)

The decision at Jerusalem was good in theory, but it is more complex in the way it is worked out in practice. The council allowed the Jewish Christians to go on living as Jews, observing circumcision and the law, whilst allowing the Gentile Christians to continue in their own culture with some social modifications. However, this raised further questions. Was the Jewish way of life a superior Christian culture to that of the Gentiles? Does the keeping of the Law make a better class of Christian?

No! argues Paul. Culture is the way of life for people. No matter how much guidance one receives from a law given by God, one will not be able to live a perfect life because of the inherent sinfulness of man. That person will not be able to obtain salvation by what he does and therefore will not be saved by following any culture, and its accompanying rules, be it Jewish or Gentile (Gal 2:16). Salvation comes only through faith in Christ. 'The life I live in the body, I live by faith in the Son of God' (verse 20).

Unity in Christ

Paul was rightly concerned about the cultural barriers that could separate Christians and goes on to discuss them with regard to baptism. In the Early Church, baptism was not merely an outward form and ceremony, but it was seen as a living illustration of union with Christ. As each person was baptised, he or she came into union with Christ, and as a result all were united with him, so all Christians were united with each other (Gal 3:26-29).

In the Jewish form of morning prayer, which Paul must have used for many years of his life, there is a thanksgiving in which the Jew thanks God that 'Thou hast not made me a Gentile, a slave or a woman.' Paul reverses this prayer to emphasise that the old distinctions have gone. In verse 28 Paul says there is now no distinction between Jew and Greek, slave and freemen, men and women: 'for you are all one in Christ Jesus.'

The unity of the Church expresses the life of Christ. When a woman becomes a Christian she is still a woman and functions biologically as a woman. Similarly, a slave is still a slave within the economic system. A Gentile remains a Gentile, and may live out his Christian life within a Gentile society. Although Paul stresses the unity we have in Christ this does not mean uniformity. A uniform culture is not the basis of our unity; however, a living relationship with the one God is.

Christian Freedom

Paul is, however, very careful that this freedom from the restraint of culture, and especially the Jewish religious culture, should not lead to immorality. Jewish law channelled people to behave in certain clearly defined ways (see figure 19:1). Now the channels are no longer necessary because the Spirit of God is living within the individual: 'So I say: live by the Spirit, and you will not gratify the desires of the sinful nature' (Gal 5:16).

The Christian is free from the limitation of a particular way of life and from a fixed set of laws. With the Spirit of God in any person, the character of God may be expressed within any culture. Even so, within any culture the Spirit will manifest through the Christian the same character of Christ, which is the fruit of the Spirit (Gal 5:22-26).

186

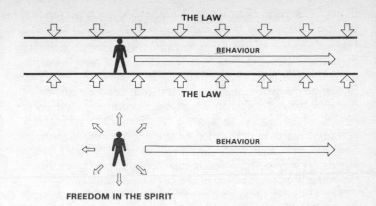

Fig 19:1
Restraint and Freedom

Gospel and Culture

Human cultures reflect human nature. As a result of the Fall, man and creation are tainted and spoilt, and yet because men and women are created by God there remains something of the nature of God. The Reformed theologians spoke of the 'total depravity of man.' (See ch 3, p36.)

This doctrine can be carried over to human cultures. The customs and culture of all people are likewise tainted. As the Lausanne Covenant states: 'Because man is God's creature, some of his culture is rich in beauty and goodness. Because he has fallen, all of it is tainted with sin and some of it is demonic.'[3]

As the Gospel enters a culture, it comes as both judge and redeemer. Many components of a culture will be brought almost unnoticed by people into their new Christian lifestyle. However, other aspects of their particular culture will be evaluated by the Gospel according to its own criteria of truth and righteousness. Some of those aspects will be rejected as incompatible with the Spirit of God. Other aspects of peoples' lives will have to be modified and transformed, while yet further aspects may go unchanged.

187

A useful illustration of this principle has been given by Donald McGavran[4] with regard to the conversion of the Naga people of Assam. The Nagas showed great hospitality to visitors, and this was recognised as good and incorporated into Christian behaviour. Other aspects of Naga culture were modified, such as the custom that the youths of the tribe would sleep in a common dormitory and there receive education in the ways and beliefs of the tribe. Now as Christians they continued to sleep in common dormitories, but were instructed in Christian ways. Finally, some aspects were rejected as being unacceptable for Christians — most notably that the Nagas had been head-hunters!

The Holy Spirit will be manifest in each culture through the establishment of the Church, and according to the precepts of Scripture. Thus the people of God become salt and light to their society. The Kingdom becomes more of a present reality within a society as the Church exerts a positive influence upon that community.

The people of God are now a multi-cultural community revealing the life of the Kingdom among all nations. One can no longer speak of a single Christian culture, but rather of a multitude of Christianised societies. It is the responsibility of every church to reveal what it means to live out the life of Christ within its own society. Christ incarnate through every church in every culture should be the aim of mission.

Discussion Questions

1 Is there such a thing as a 'Christian culture'? Explain your answer.
2 To what extent and in what ways should Christians differ from their culture?

Recommended Reading

Thom Hopler, *A World of Difference* (IVP: Leicester, 1981).
Donald McGavran, *The Clash Between Christianity and Cultures* (Canon Press: Washington, 1974).

Lausanne Commission for World Evangelisation *Explaining the Gospel in Today's World* (Scripture Union: London, 1978).

Footnotes

1   Marvin K Mayers, *Christianity Confronts Culture* (Zondervan: Michigan, 1974) p 227.

2   James quotes from the Septuagint, which suggests that the proceedings were conducted in the Greek language for the sake of the Gentile Christians present. The Septuagint translation of Amos 9:11-12 differs considerably from the traditional Hebrew Text.

3   J D Douglas, 'The Lausanne Covenant' *Let the Earth Hear His Voice* (World Wide Publications: Minneapolis, 1974) p 6.

4   Donald McGavran, *The Clash Between Christianity and Cultures* (Canon Press: Washington, 1974) pp 38-42.

20

THE QUESTION
OF ISRAEL

*People ask me why I am a Jew. It is to you that I want to
answer, little unborn grandson . . .*

*I am a Jew because, born of Israel and having lost her, I
have felt her live again in me, more living than myself.*

*I am a Jew because, born of Israel and having regained her,
I wish her to live after me, more living than in myself.*

*I am a Jew because the faith of Israel demands of me no
abdication of the mind.*

*I am a Jew because in every place where suffering weeps, the
Jew weeps.*

*I am a Jew because at every time when despair cries out, the
Jew hopes.*

*I am a Jew because the word of Israel is the oldest and the
newest.*

*I am a Jew because the promise of Israel is the universal
promise.*

*I am a Jew because, for Israel, the world is not yet completed;
men are completing it.*

*I am a Jew because, above the nations and Israel, Israel
places Man and his Unity.*

*I am a Jew because, above Man, image of the divine Unity,
Israel places the divine Unity, and its divinity . . .*

*And I say to myself: From this remote father (Abraham) right
up to my own father, all these fathers have handed on to me a
truth which flowed in their blood, which flows in mine; and
shall I not hand it on, with my blood, to those of my blood?*

*Will you take it from me, my child? Will you hand it on?
Perhaps you will wish to abandon it. If so, let it be for a greater
truth, if there is one. I shall not blame you. It will be my fault; I
shall have failed to hand it on as I received it.*[1]

Throughout the Old Testament God's redemptive work is occurring through the Hebrew people, but with the birth of the Church the emphasis shifts. What continuing purposes did God have for the people of Israel? Was Israel merely to become part of the new multi-cultural people of God?

By the time Paul wrote Romans in about 58 AD, it was becoming clear that the Jews were not responding to the Gospel of the Kingdom. If the purposes of God were now to be achieved through the Church, why was it that the Jews failed to realise what God was doing? The Jews should have been the very people who responded most readily to the new work of God, and yet the Gentiles were accepting its truth. Had the promises of God failed?

Mission in Romans

All too often the epistle to the Romans is regarded as a theological textbook which is the sole prerogative of the theologian. Paul, however, was not just some 'ivory tower' theologian, but a missionary with very clear missionary goals, as we must remember when we consider the reason why this letter was written.

Traditional explanations of the purpose of the letter have tended to see it as the full statement of Paul's doctrinal beliefs. Certainly, Paul develops some of the great theological truths in this letter, such as those about sin, justification, and sanctification, but there are many important truths missing, such as those concerning eschatology. The personal comments show that Paul had a more immediate and practical objective.

A number of writers[2] have tended to regard the section from chapter 9-11 as being no more than a digression in the main text. This view cannot be accepted because the issues considered in the section chapters 9-11 contain some questions of vital importance to Paul such as the sovereignty of God as related to Israel. One senses a passionate concern in these verses which stress their importance. I would suggest, though, that the key in understanding the missionary significance of Romans lies in chapter 15: 20-24. 'It has always been my ambition to proclaim the Gospel where Christ was

191

not known, so that I would not be building on someone else's foundation . . . I plan to do so when I go to Spain. I hope to visit you while passing through and to have you assist me on my journey there, after I have enjoyed your company for a while.'

Paul saw the opportunity of taking the Gospel to the western part of the Roman Empire, but to achieve this he would need a base further west than Ephesus. Rome would be the ideal place to see the Gospel move west to Gaul, Spain and North Africa.

This missionary thrust gives a unity to the letter. Paul writes Gospel truths which lead logically to the commission of taking this Gospel to all people. Chapters 9-11 now take on an important significance in answering the question which must have perplexed many Gentile converts, as well as Paul himself. Why were the Jews not responding to the Gospel? Today the missionary frequently faces the question of why certain people are responsive to the Gospel and others are resistant. Here within these chapters one finds at least part of the answer.

God's Sovereignty

One should not underestimate Paul's great sorrow at the fact that the Jews were not responding to the Gospel in any great number: 'For I could wish that I myself were cursed and cut off from Christ' (Rom 9:3). Paul was willing to be damned if his people, the Jews, could be saved. This is the same unselfish love one finds in many missionaries through the history of Christianity. David Brainard, who worked amongst the North American Indians, once prayed: 'Damn me if they will be saved.'

Paul's answer as to why the Jews have not responded is founded upon the fact that God is sovereign. The question of why God chooses to elect some and not others lies within the purposes of God. It is not for the missionary to question God, but it is for the missionary to feel compassion for all people because God would have all people come to salvation.

Even in accepting the sovereignty of God many questions arise, and Paul finds an answer to these in a proper understanding of the character of God himself.

Is God Unfaithful? (Rom 9: 6-13)

Does not the fact that the people of Israel are not responding show that God is unfaithful to his promises? Paul answers by showing that although God's promise was given to Abraham and his 'seed', it was not for all his children. Abraham had eight children from three different women, and yet it was only through Isaac that the promise could be fulfilled. Genesis 21:12 is quoted to underline this point. The children of Abraham who received the promise were those who shared his faith, not his blood.

Similarly with the twin sons of Rebecca, God was at work through the events in their lives. According to Hebrew culture Esau should have inherited the promise, but God chose Jacob. These two men were differentiated not on the grounds of their life or character, but totally by the choice of God.

The names Jacob and Esau must be interpreted in the sense of nations, not individuals, which is the original context of the Old Testament quotations (Gen 25:23; Mal 1:2, 3). 'Love' and 'hate' are not subjective feelings, but emotional terms used to indicate the function and destiny of these two peoples. Judah, not Edom, was elected for God's purpose of progressive revelation in history.

Is God Unjust? (Rom 9: 14-21)

Accepting that God is not unfaithful, the logical consequence is to ask whether God is therefore unjust. Why should he choose one, and not the other? Paul answers by directing the questioner to realise who he is, and who God is. No one deserves to be saved. No one can demand the right to be chosen. It is not a matter of justice, but of mercy. Paul uses the illustration of the potter to press home the point. When the potter picks up the clay and puts it on his wheel, what right does the clay have to say into what sort of vessel it should be made?

God has a right to manage our lives in the way he wills. Paul is not here arguing the sovereignty of God or the free will of man, but the free will of God. Let God be God! One may not understand predestination, nor even like it, but God is fair. God need not choose anyone, but he has chosen some to whom to show his mercy, and others to whom to demonstrate his power and wrath. Today's missionary must be aware of this sombre truth.

Is God Unpredictable? (Rom 9:22-29)

If God chose Israel in the Old Testament, and now in this new era he rejects Israel, does that not make him unpredictable? Once again, Paul's answer is 'No!' Some 700 years before, God had promised through his prophets that he would do just this (Isa 10:22-23; Hos 2:23; 1:10). The sovereignty of God is a basic principle within the mission of the Church. From a human point of view it stands as one side of a paradox which through the history of the Church has caused much argument.

If one accepts the fact that God is sovereign and his decrees are unchanging, it therefore means that the elect must be saved. Does this mean that evangelism is unnecessary? God is Almighty, and if he wished he could save all the elect by a sheer act of his power. However, God has chosen not to use compulsion to bring any person to himself. God deals with human beings as rational, moral creatures who are free agents. Therefore he reasons and pleads with the unsaved through the presentation of the Gospel. The means that God uses to bring the elect to salvation are as important as the ultimate aims that he has for them.

Thus as R B Kuiper, a leading Reformed theologian writes: 'A most significant conclusion is now warranted. Instead of rendering evangelism superfluous, election demands evangelism. All of God's elect must be saved. Not one of them may perish.'[3] The fact of divine sovereignty needs to be balanced by the contrasting aspect of human responsibility.

The Problem for Israel

Paul now turns to address the question of Israel's attitude to God, and in so doing contrasts the two ways of viewing God. The way followed by the Jews was one of seeking to set oneself right with God by effort. Religious zeal, however sincere, is not enough in its own right. To gain God's approval by effort a person must be perfect.

The significance of this fact in the consideration of the Christian attitude to other religions is very important. If God made such demands from his people in the practice which he had clearly revealed to them in the Old Testament, how much more will this be true of people of any other religion in the world? If the Jews could not achieve this perfection, even though God had intervened so much in their culture, then neither may adherents of any other religion.

The alternative way of approaching God is by faith. 'For it is with your heart that you believe and are justified, and it is with your mouth that you confess and are saved' (Rom 10:10). The Jews were rejected because they sought to gain God's approval by their own effort, and they were therefore judged on that basis, and found wanting.

The Universal Proclamation

God's provision is the way of faith: 'Everyone who calls on the name of the Lord will be saved' (Rom 10:13). From this point Paul leads the reader through a series of brief statements to the inevitable conclusion. He says people need to call on the Lord, thus they need to hear about the Lord, and therefore must be told about the Lord. Hence the need for mission: 'Consequently, faith comes from hearing the message, and the message is heard through the word of Christ' (Rom 10:17).

But, how does this apply to the Jews? Did they not hear the message? 'Of course they did' says Paul (verse 18). Did they then not understand? Isaiah says: 'Yes, they heard and understood, but they rejected God's message' (Rom 10:20 GNB). Paul therefore concludes that the Jews have no excuse. Today we are faced with an additional question:

What about the many people who have never heard and have never understood the message?

The Question of Those Who Have Never Heard

Paul does not give an answer to this question, but it has perplexed Christians down through history. It presents the missionary with one of the most difficult and agonising questions. Among evangelicals various views have been suggested,[4] three of which are most widely held.

One states that man is a sinner and as such is completely lost. Salvation comes only through faith in Christ, and unless a person responds to the invitation of the Gospel he is condemned. No distinction is therefore made between those who have heard the Gospel and rejected it, and those who have never heard it. The people are both in the same situation and face the same fate.

Others argue that even though people may be ignorant of the Gospel, they still have the light revealed by God in creation and providence, as well as their conscience (Rom 1:20-23; 2:14-15; Acts 14:17). Those who have never heard of Christ will be judged according to the light of their conscience. The Jews on the other hand will be judged by the light of the Law, and those who know the Gospel by the light of the Gospel. However, it may be asked whether those who have never heard can actually live up to the light they have received. To this the answer would appear to be negative from such verses as Romans 3:23: 'for all have sinned and fall short of the glory of God'.

A third group would answer the question by first asking whether men of God in the Old Testament will be saved. They were deficient in knowledge but were nevertheless forgiven by grace through faith, as seen in Hebrews chapter 11. Those who argue in this way draw a parallel between Old Testament Israelites and those who have never heard. They would thus argue that God will surely judge those who have never heard by the response they would have made if they had heard.[5]

The question will undoubtedly continue to perplex the Church. The danger of the latter view is that it takes away something of the urgency of mission, although recognising the gracious character of God. One thing in fact is clear from Scripture: that the Judge of all will judge with righteousness.

God's Mercy
In the midst of this great discourse on the sovereignty of God, Paul does not want his readers to fail in appreciating the great mercy of God.

To Israel
There is always a danger of exaggeration. Did God reject his own people? No, argues Paul. Many of the Jews have been incorporated into the people of God. The old branches that have been cut away are the Jews who have refused to accept the Gospel.

This is indeed an unusual grafting, but one in which both the graft and the root stock are reinvigorated. The new graft is able to draw upon the sap of the olive stock, and so is able to bear fruit more abundantly than the original stock. For the Gentiles this should not lead to pride or any sense of superiority over the Jews, but a sense of awe at what God has done.

To All
Paul now leads on to the very heart of God's purpose for Israel, and such perception could only have come through some specific revelation. Paul reveals the fact that the stubbornness of Israel is only partial, and a time will come when Israel will respond to the Gospel. When the full number of Gentiles has come to God, then all Israel will be saved (Rom 11:25, 26). In order that the Gentiles might come in, and the universal purposes of the Gospel be fulfilled, the Jews had to be put to one side. But this is only for a time. They are God's people, and they have a special place in the plan of God.

Revelation chapter 7 has been the object of many exotic interpretations, but one point is clear — that God has not forgotten his ancient people. There will be those from each of the 12 tribes of Israel among the redeemed. God's ultimate purpose for the world is now revealed and will include both Jew and Gentile alike. No wonder Paul ends the section with a doxology of worship. God will indeed fulfil his purposes perfectly.

Discussion Questions

1 Does the fact that God is sovereign mean that the Christian need not evangelise?

2 If a Jew becomes a Christian would you advise him to give up his Jewish way of life? What place would the Law of Moses have in how he leads his life?

3 Which people will be saved? What is the fate of those who have never heard the Gospel? What clues does Paul give in Romans to help us approach and answer this difficult question?

4 Paul's ambition was to proclaim the Good News in places where Christ had not been heard of (Rom 15:20). What is your ambition?

Recommended Reading

F F Bruce, *Romans* (Tyndale Press: London, 1963).

Stuart Olyott, *The Gospel As It Really Is* (Evangelical Press: Welwyn, 1979).

Gordon Jessup, *No Strange God* (Olive Press: London, 1976).

Lance Lambert, *The Uniqueness of Israel* (Kingsway: Eastbourne, 1980).

Footnotes

1 Edmond Fleg, 'Why I am a Jew', in *The Zionist Idea*, Arthur Hertzberg, editor (Doubleday: New York, 1959) pp 481-485.

2 C I Schofield, *Holy Bible* (Oxford University Press: Oxford, 1945), p 1191.

3 R B Kuiper, *God-Centred Evangelism* (The Banner of Truth: London, 1961) p 38.

4 Malcolm McVeigh, 'The Fate of Those Who've Never Heard? It Depends', *Evangelical Missions Quarterly* Vol 21, No 4 (1985): pp 372-379.

5 J N D Anderson, *Christianity and World Religions: The Challenge of Pluralism* (IVP: Leicester, 1984).

21

THE KINGDOM COMMUNITY AND THE WORLD RELIGIONS

Krishna lived with his wife and two sons and a daughter in a little village in Nepal. He and his family were Hindus. One morning, their four-year-old daughter became sick and within a short time she was dead. Four months later Krishna came to the Christians saying that Hinduism had done nothing for his family, and he wanted to become a follower of the one true living God. He had already thrown out all of the family idols and had refused to offer any more sacrifices. Krishna knew almost nothing about Jesus Christ, but he and his family now wanted to follow him. They had only one problem. What about their little daughter through whose death they had turned to the true God? Would she be saved as he and his family turned to Christ?[1]

As the Church in the first century quickly began to expand into the different societies that made up the Roman Empire, many issues arose. First, as we have just seen, were the considerations of how the multi-cultural Christian community could relate to the traditions of Israel. Secondly, questions also arose as to how the new Gentile converts should consider their former religions. Similar issues face the Church today. How does the Christian view those of other faiths? To what extent does Christian mission require a Hindu, Muslim or Buddhist to renounce his traditional faith?

200

Traditional Attitudes to Other Religions

The religions of the Roman Empire in the first century can be described as animism, or more preferably as primal religions. Burnett Tylor coined the term 'animism' for those who believe that the universe is populated with spirits who can have a direct influence upon humanity, for good or evil.[2] The expression 'primal religions' is used to describe those which were in existence before the expansion of the major world religions and were basically tribal religions unique to a particular people. A world religion, on the other hand, purports to be universal and so spreads beyond one particular people. In general, the world religions have usually originated from a tribal religion, and developed into a universal religion embracing many peoples. As we have seen, Christianity has grown out of Judaism, and in so doing has taken on a broader, multi-cultural appeal.

As Christianity became multi-cultural, it showed itself able to accommodate the way of life of various peoples. However, with regard to their loyalty to the Christian faith and the rejection of other gods, the Early Church was uncompromising. The early Christians were regarded as atheists by the Roman authorities because they would not worship the accepted Roman gods, which included the Emperor himself. Hence the Early Church suffered several major persecutions as a result of their stubbornness in worshipping none other than the Lord.

Later, the Roman Catholic Church was to emphasise the view that salvation is only found in the Church. As was stated at the Council of Florence (1438-45), 'The holy Roman Church believes, professes and proclaims that none of those who are outside the Church — not only pagan, but Jews also, heretics and schismatics — can have part in eternal life, but will go to the eternal fire "which was prepared for the devil and his angels", unless they are gathered into that Church before the end of life.'[3]

Other religions were regarded as emanating not from God, but from Satan. The presence of other religions in the world was regarded as no more than the work of the enemy to blind men against the need to come to an understanding of the truth. Most Roman Catholic theologians would react against such an extreme view today. As from the Vatican II Conference (1964) there has been a variety of views, which will be mentioned later.

The Protestant equivalent to the traditional Roman position is that salvation is only found within Christianity. The converse therefore becomes true: that no one outside of Christianity can be saved — all are condemned to hell. This therefore raises the entire question of who will be saved. Most theologians have in general reacted away from these traditional approaches and have sought what they would consider more acceptable views of understanding other religions of the world.

Modern Approaches to World Religions
At least four main approaches to other religions have been at the centre of debate within this century.

Fulfilment A strong reaction to the view that other religions were of the Devil occurred at the beginning of this century with what became known as the 'fulfilment school'. The most well known writer of this school is J N Farquhar, who in his book *The Crown of Hinduism*[4] claimed that Christ came to fulfil Hinduism in a similar way to how he had fulfilled the Law and the Prophets (Matt 5). It is to be noted that it is Christ, not Christianity, who is the fulfilment of Hinduism.

This view argues that no religious system ever contains the total truth because all are based upon human effort and are therefore inadequate. No religion in itself can ever save a person, and Jesus is needed as the final revelation. God's purpose in Christ was therefore to make up the deficiency of any particular religious system. This led Farquhar to write, 'Jesus Christ is the crown of Hinduism'.

This view is popular with many scholars associated with the World Council of Churches as it provides a viable basis for dialogue between Christians and those of other faiths.

Discontinuity In preparation for the 1938 conference at Tambaram (nr Madras), the Dutch scholar Hendrick Kraemer was invited to put forward his view of radical discontinuity in opposition to the 'fulfilment' approach. Kraemer's book *The Christian Message in a Non-Christian World*[5] can still be read with great profit.

Kraemer argued that there was a radical 'discontinuity' (a term he coined) between Christianity and other religions. Christianity was not a fulfilment of any religion nor an extension of it, apart from Judaism. He concluded that all other religions are merely men's attempts to build their own religious system. They are therefore either idolatry, or an attempt to justify oneself by good works. They are all therefore bound to fail.

Correlations Following Kraemer's thesis, there was much discussion, especially within the World Council of Churches (WCC). An important contribution to the debate was that of Paul Tillich,[6] who argued that all religions co-operate with the Gospel, and so in this way support it. The result is that all religions lead men to the 'ground of being'.

This view states the nature of God is revealed in such a way that God reaches men through all other religions. The major contribution of Christianity is then considered to be the manifestation of God as a God of love, and we can therefore know that he accepts all humankind. A person may be hostile to Christianity, or even to Jesus Christ as he knows him, but if he is a sincere devotee of his own religion, he is accepted by God — his very sincerity is said to make him acceptable. God receives the worship of all men independent of religion, and independent of the name by which he is called.

Manifestations Since the Second Vatican Council, Roman Catholic scholars have shown a great deal of interest in the subject of inter-religious dialogue. One of the most influential concepts has been that of 'the anonymous Christian', proposed by Karl Rahner.[7] Rahner's argument has been clearly stated by Peter Cotterell as follows:

If God wills all men to be saved, and if the majority of

mankind is allied to the non-Christian religions, and if salvation is only to be found in Christ, then, Christ must somehow be at work in these religions, by grace.[8]

In the words of Rahner himself, '[Salvation is] not only for Christians, but for all men of good will in whose hearts grace works in an unseen way. For, since Christ died for all men, and since the ultimate vocation of man is in fact one, and divine, we ought to believe that the Holy Spirit in a manner known only to God offers to every man the possibility of being associated with this paschal mystery.'[9]

These 'anonymous Christians' are saved not by their natural morality but because they have experienced the grace of Jesus Christ without realising the fact. Christianity therefore should not merely approach a member of another religion as a non-Christian, but as someone who must be recognised as an 'anonymous Christian', and respected as such. Mission therefore is the bringing into the explicit consciousness of the individual what God has already done implicitly.

A study of these four modern approaches reveals that the main division of opinion relates to whether there exists a continuity or a discontinuity, to use Kraemer's expression, between Christianity and other religions. This is the heart of the debate. All groups assume that a continuity exists between Judaism and Christianity, but that is outside the current topic. However, is Christianity totally unique from other religions? Is there any continuity of Christianity with other religions or not? One's answer to this question vitally affects one's whole concept and method of mission. If we assume, on the one hand, that there is a continuity between Christianity and other religions, one will see mission only as an interaction with other human beings in order to share, and gain from each others' religious experience to the mutual benefit of all. But if, on the other hand, we assume that there is a discontinuity, one of the aims of mission must be to bring people of other religions to where they reject those religions as of no value for salvation.

Christianity – a Unique Religion?

Having examined the traditional and more recent attitudes to other religions, we must now turn to the repercussions of these ideas in the context of Scripture.

A Unique Gospel

The Old Testament makes a clear distinction between the religion of Yahweh and that of the surrounding nations, as was considered in a previous chapter discussing the power encounter between Yahweh and Baal (pp84–86). The prophets made it clear that Israel must remain distinct from the surrounding nations. However, can it now be argued that with the coming of the multi-cultural Church, the movement from the specific to the universal reaches its ultimate in the embracing of all peoples and religions? Is the Old Testament rejection of other religions now superceded by universal salvation?

At the outset, we must emphasise that the New Testament does not replace the Old, but confirms and fulfils it. The New Testament writers also reject the validity of salvation in other religions. For example, Paul writes to the Ephesians, 'at that time you were separate from Christ, excluded from citizenship in Israel and foreigners to the covenants of the promise, without hope and without God in the world' (Eph 2:12). There is no suggestion in this passage that somehow before the Ephesians came to Christ they had any awareness of the God of the Scriptures. This would illustrate the basis of Kraemer's argument of discontinuity.

Does this then mean that the non-Christian is therefore totally abandoned by God? It must be agreed that such a view is unacceptable. Throughout the Old Testament one sees God's concern has been for all people, and not just his own chosen people. God sends rain on the just and unjust. God reveals himself to all men through his creation: 'For since the creation of the world God's invisible qualities – his eternal power and divine nature – have been clearly seen' (Rom 1:20). There are not just two options; God present with his people, and God abandoning others in godlessness and hopelessness. There is a third option, God at work amongst all the nations of the world to fulfil his purposes, and man having the freedom to respond or to reject his offer.

The Issue of Unknown Gods

Is not mission therefore just what Rahner has said, the raising in people's consciousness of what is already there implicitly? Is this not what Paul does in Acts 17:22, 23 when he speaks to the Athenians, 'I see that in every way you are very religious. For as I walked around and observed your objects of worship, I even found an altar with this inscription: "To an Unknown God." Now what you worship as something unknown, I am going to proclaim to you.'

Paul, however, is not here complimenting them for their religiousness, but underscoring the fact of their ignorance. This is a rather subtle exposure of the inadequacy of polytheism rather than any approval of their religion. In polytheistic societies it is common for people to believe in 'unknown god(s)'. If you believe in the possibility of many gods then there is always the possibility of a god of whom you have never heard. You therefore give offerings to such a god to ensure against possible harm from a neglected deity.

Paul emphasises that God is not like their gods. 'God . . . does not live in temples built by hands' (Acts 17:24), nor is he 'served by human hands . . .' (verse 25). 'We should not think that the divine being is like gold or silver or stone . . .' (verse 29). Likewise, the Christians of the Early Church were adamant in their refusal to compromise with idolatry even if it meant death. This was more than a holdover from the Jewish past. It is a clear directive to the whole Church. 'You turned to God from idols, to serve the living and true God, and to wait for his Son from heaven' (I Thes 1:9-10).

Although Paul refutes other religions, he nevertheless is respectful to those who hold other beliefs. For example when Paul is before the rioting crowd in Ephesus, the town clerk makes the telling statement, 'You have brought these men here, though they have neither robbed temples nor blasphemed our goddess' (Acts 19:37). Likewise we need to be gracious and respect the religious views of others, even if we do not agree with them.

Redemptive Analogies

Paul does actually quote from a pagan hymn in his proclamation to the Athenians (Acts 17:28). However, Paul uses the quote by way of an illustration of the truth rather than as the truth itself. Man as a creature of God living within a world created by God, in spite of the Fall, has a certain awareness of the truth. All religious systems must, to a greater or lesser extent, have some element which points towards the true God. Certainly, this is mixed with much which may be un-Christian or even demonic, but God has not left himself without a witness.

Don Richardson[10] has argued that within every society there is some analogy which is helpful to a people in understanding the Gospel message. This is dramatically illustrated by the *Peace Child*[11] story from Irian Jaya. Here a traditional cultural practice provides the illustration for the Sarwi people to appreciate the role of Christ as God's 'peace child' for humankind.

The analogy which is used may be a myth, a ritual, or a custom practised by the people. It is more than a mere illustration, but it is an actual belief or practice of the people. In this way the truth of the Gospel is communicated in ways that people are readily able to comprehend; the analogy leads not to compromise but to redemption.

By What Authority?

To assume that Christianity provides the only means of salvation may sound to many like fanaticism and religious imperialism. The claim of Paul that the Athenians are ignorant in their religion while he is going to proclaim to them the truth, sounds like bigotry. How can a man be so bold in his proclamation? This note of authority is common among the apostles, as it was of Jesus himself. The key to the understanding of apostolic authority is that it is delegated messianic authority. They presented their teaching as Christ's truth, Spirit-given, in both content and form of expression. That is why they could speak with such confidence, because they were Christ's commissioned witnesses and ambassadors (II Cor 5:20).

Not a Religion, but a Person

The apostles were not comparing one religious system with another. To compare Christianity as a religious system with that of Islam or Hinduism is to fail to understand the heart of the Gospel message. The Good News of the Kingdom is the Lord Jesus Christ himself, who is the King.

Religious systems are all human responses, and as such they contain human and even demonic elements. Man-made empires have been constructed even within the established Church, and these have often been the very opposite of what the Kingdom should be. Jesus told his disciples that an enemy would sow weeds in the harvest field. The *euangelion* is Jesus Christ himself, and not the Christian religion with all its cultural attributes.

Discussion Questions

1 What about those who have never heard of Christ? Do you think that they will be condemned, or will they be judged on their response to the 'light' they have received? (Ps 58:11; Ps 1:5; Acts 4:12; Rom 2:6, 7)
2 Do you agree with the author's conclusion that sincerity in one's religion is not sufficient to please God?
3 Is it right to use the Qur'an in order to illustrate the message of Christianity? What are the uses and dangers?
4 Consider one major world religion. What points of agreement do you find in it with Christianity?

Recommended Reading

H Kraemer, *The Christian Message in a Non-Christian World* (Edinburgh House Press: Edinburgh, 1938).
Stephen Neil, *Christian Faiths and Other Faiths* (Oxford University Press: Oxford, 1970).
Don Richardson, *Eternity in Their Hearts* (Regal Books: Ventura, Ca, 1981).

Dick Dowsett, *God, That's Not Fair* (OMF Books: Seven-oaks, 1982).
Kenneth F W Prior, *The Gospel in a Pagan Society* (Hodder & Stoughton: London, 1975).

Footnotes

1 Private comment to author.

2 E Burnett Tylor, *Primitive Cultures* (John Murray: London, 1871) pp 425-27.

3 Hans Kung, *On Being a Christian* (Collins: London, 1977) p 97.

4 J N Farquhar, *The Crown of Hinduism* (Oxford University Press: Madras, 1915).

5 Hendrick Kraemer, *The Christian Message in a Non-Christian World* (The Edinburgh House Press: London 1938).

6 Paul Tillich, *Christianity & the Encounter of the World Religions* (Columbia University Press: New York, 1963).

7 Karl Rahner, *Theological Investigations* Vol 5 (Darton, Longman & Todd: London, 1954).

8 Peter Cotterell, *The Eleventh Commandment* (IVP: Leicester, 1981) pp 11-16.

9 Quoted in Tony Lane, *The Lion Concise Book of Christian Thought* (Lion Publishing: Tring, 1984) p 218.

10 Don Richardson, *Eternity in Their Heart* (Regal Books: Ventura, 1981).

11 Don Richardson, *Peace Child* (Gospel Light/Regal Books: Glendale, 1974).

22

WAR IN THE HEAVENS

'Can you kill that goat without touching it?' The witch-doctor challenged me, pointing to a goat standing nearby. I had just told him of the death of Christ on the cross and suddenly he turned to me with the above question.

His claim was that he could kill with his fetish power. I told him that I knew a greater power, that of Jesus who can give life to the spiritually dead. 'Would you let me pray for you?' I asked him. 'Yes, but let me pray for you first,' he replied. I took his hand. He 'prayed' in a language which I did not understand. But I felt in my heart that he was trying to put a curse on me. I knew also that this curse had no power over me as I was protected by the blood of Jesus.

When he had finished praying I began to pray. But he pulled his hand away from mine and shouted, 'No, don't pray for me.' I knew that he was aware that my prayer could adversely affect his fetish power. He preferred to keep his black power rather than submit to the life-giving power of Jesus.[1]

An important aspect of the missionary nature of the Church is that which relates to the unseen world. This was an aspect clearly recognised by Christ during his earthly ministry, and is evident amongst his apostles in their mission. John writes, 'The reason the Son of God appeared was to destroy the devil's work (I John 3:8). Paul mentions this aspect in every one of his epistles apart from Philemon. It is therefore surprising that this dimension is frequently neglected in the theology of mission.

The Unseen World

During the early part of this century there was much scepticism about the existence of that part of creation which we may generally call the 'unseen'. Western materialism was not only questioning the existence of God, but the whole of that which is outside the natural order. If something could not be observed, measured, and studied, its very existence was denied.

In recent years, this view has been changing for several reasons. First, during the Nazi period, German theologians saw ordinary people perpetrate such terrible acts of cruelty that they could only be described as demonic. Secondly, Western philosphy showed a marked move from that of closed materialism to that of existentialism. Existentialism places an emphasis not on the objective mechanical nature of the universe, but on the subjective experience of the individual. In recent years this has led to an increasing interest, especially among young people, in the occult, paranormal phenomena, and in the cults. It is the subjective experience which is now believed to be of paramount importance by many in the Western world. A third reason has been the growth of the Pentecostal and Charismatic movements within the Western Church. Both groups have placed great emphasis upon the exercise of supernatural gifts and on divine healing.

In seeking to understand the 'unseen world', we must first appreciate several principles:

God created the unseen All religions recognise the existence of an 'other world', or a supernatural world in which various gods and spirits exist. The Bible similarly speaks about a supernatural world and supernatural beings. This essential theme runs throughout the whole of the Scriptures. What is more, this supernatural world is part of God's created order. Paul makes that quite explicit in Colossians: 'For by him all things were created: things in heaven and on earth, visible and invisible, whether thrones or powers or rulers or authorities; all things were created by him and for him' (Col 1:16).

This is a logical consequence of the Genesis assertion that

God is the one and only Creator, and nothing existed along-side him before the Creation. If God created the unseen it must initially have been very good, a part of God's whole purpose for his Creation. Charles Kraft[2] has proposed the model shown in figure 22:1, to describe the biblical classification of living beings. Apart from God who alone is absolute, there are the created beings which are classed as angels, whether or not they are fallen, and humans. Culture is basically a human activity, and so the angels together with God are classified as supracultural. It is the supracultural which makes up the 'unseen world'.

The unseen affects the seen Throughout the whole of the Scriptures the influence of the unseen upon the seen is continually recognised, although the concepts employed do show some variation. Genesis 6:2: 'The sons of God saw that the daughters of men were beautiful, and they married any of them they chose.' 'There the angel of the Lord appeared to him in flames of fire from within a bush' (Exod 3:2). 'One day the angels came to present themselves before the Lord, and Satan also came with them. The Lord said to Satan, "Where have you come from?" Satan answered the Lord, "From roaming through the earth and going to and fro in it"' (Job 1:6, 7).

This awareness of the supernatural and its influence upon humankind was not only a major issue in the worldview of the peoples of the ancient Middle East but is also important among many peoples in the world today.

There is a state of war Within the unseen world exists what the Bible describes as a war, a conflict between two opposing forces. Jesus on numerous occasions speaks about an adversary who ultimately will be defeated. 'Jesus answered them, "I saw Satan fall like lightning from heaven"' (Luke 10:18) 'But if I drive out demons by the finger of God, then the kingdom of God has come to you' (Luke 11:20).

This state of war affects the whole of God's creation, including the material world. The origin of the Fall itself is placed in the realms of the unseen from which temptation first came. The Kingdom concept reveals a coming of a new Kingdom into the world, and at the interface of these two

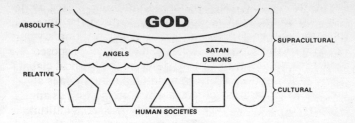

Fig 22:1

Modification of Kraft's Analysis of God's
Creation of the Supernatural

opposing Kingdoms is conflict. Mission therefore takes place within this spiritual conflict.

Principalities and Powers
The major question for the Western Christian is, 'Do these spiritual forces actually exist, or is Jesus just relating himself to the thought patterns of the people of his day and culture?' In our scientific Western worldview we are able to explain many of these phenomena in terms of psychological or physio-chemical phenomena. However, is this Western understanding correct? If Jesus came to the world today, would he still use the same concepts of devils and demons?

Assuming that one accepts the divinity of Jesus one must find the materialistic worldview — common to our Western society — unacceptable for several reasons. First, Jesus did not indiscriminately take over all the views of his age. His views on many issues were totally contrary to those of his culture and thus led him into conflict with the leaders of his society. His views on money, divorce, the Sabbath, and forgiveness were all different. Why should Jesus conform to the ideas of his culture on the particular aspect of the demonic?

Secondly, the whole ministry of healing and exorcism is central to Christ's mission in inaugurating the kingdom of God. To take away the motif of a conflict with Satan diminishes the basis of the ministry of Jesus.

213

Thirdly, the materialistic philosophy which denies the existence of the supernatural is generally limited to the Western world, whereas throughout much of the Third World a belief in the powers of evil is firmly held even today. Could the problem be not so much with the teaching Jesus, but with our Western worldview which finds it so difficult to accept the notion of the supernatural? William Irwin Thompson has said, 'We are like flies crawling across the ceiling of the Sistine Chapel. We cannot see what angels and gods lie underneath the threshold of our perception.'[3] Either our worldview must change to accept the teaching of Jesus, or we must hold on grimly to our ethnocentric superiority.

Dr Martin Lloyd-Jones in his important work on *The Christian Warfare* has written:

> The Modern world, and especially the history of the present century, can only be understood in terms of the unusual activity of the devil and the 'principalities and powers' of darkness. Indeed, I suggest that belief in the personal devil and demon activities is the touchstone by which one can most easily test any profession of Christian faith today . . . In a world of collapsing institutions, moral chaos, and increasing violence, never was it more important to trace the hand of 'the prince of the power of the air' . . . If we cannot discern the chief cause of our ills how can we hope to cure them?[4]

Satan and His Powers

The New Testament writers use many names for the forces of evil. These include principalities, powers, thrones, dominions, lords, princes, spirits, angels, and elemental spirits (Greek *stoicheia*). Satan is also given many synonyms such as the devil, the serpent, the lion, the tempter, the accuser, the enemy, the liar, the murderer, the god of this age, and Beelzebub. In spite of the numerous terms, the overall picture throughout Scripture is basically the same. One sees varied forces of evil under a unified head. The Bible does not give details as to the origin and organisation of these powers, but it does command that they should be resisted.

Two major confusions concerning the biblical view have been prevalent in recent years. The first has been whether Satan is to be perceived as a person, or as the personification of a general force of evil which influences the world. Personality is always a difficult concept when speaking of what is other than human. For example, in speaking of God as being a person this does not mean that he has the limitations of human personality. Similarly, when one speaks of Satan as being a person, it is important to realise that he is different from humanity, but he does have freedom of choice and the will to act which are the basic differences between personality and that which is impersonal. For this reason the Bible continually refers to Satan by the masculine article.

The second confusion is to see these spiritual powers as solely corrupt states or class structures. It is in this way that the teaching of Jesus has been interpreted by liberation theologians (see chapter 6). The modern preoccupation with unjust social structures should not detract from the fact that the Scriptures clearly speak of these demonic forces as being other-worldly. Even so, the Bible does relate these forces to the world. Satan is called the 'ruler of this world' (John 12:31, 14:30, 16:11). If this is the case it would be logical for both Satan and his princes to dominate not only men, but nations and ideologies.[5] The influence of Satan must not be restricted either to demonising influences on an individual – in such things as spirit possession – nor to that of sinful social structures. The Bible speaks of the influence of the demonic throughout the whole of human life, bringing about its corrupting influence.

Christ Victorious

I John 3:8 stressed that the very reason for the coming of Jesus was to destroy the works of Satan. At every point in his ministry we see Christ confronted with the forces of evil. With the temptation in the wilderness, through the many encounters with demonised people, to the final climax of his

215

death upon the cross, Christ is faced with the opposition of Satan. 'And having disarmed the powers and authorities, he made a public spectacle of them, triumphing over them by the Cross (Col 2:15). At Calvary the principalities and powers were defeated, and upon that victory is the basis of the mission of the Church.

Spiritual Warfare

The Church needs to rediscover the concept of spiritual warfare in its approach to mission. If we do not believe in the reality of principalities and powers, how can we be involved within the conflict of which Jesus speaks with regards to his ministry. As Paul writes: 'For our struggle is not against flesh and blood but against the rulers, against the authorities, against the powers of the dark world and against the spiritual forces of evil in the heavenly realms' (Eph 6:12).

The failure to recognise this aspect within Christian mission has been highlighted by Paul Hiebert.[6] He was particularly concerned with a correct understanding of traditional forms of Hinduism as found in many of the villages of South India. He drew a distinction between the seen (empirical) and the unseen (supernatural), and between the other-worldly and the worldly. (See figure 22:2.) This results in a model which has three layers: the lower relates to seen things which are observable and material, and may be manipulated by technological skills. The middle layer consists of those supernatural forces which influence this world and would include spirits, ghosts, and gods. The upper layer consists of those supernatural entities related to some transcendent deity. It deals with questions of the ultimate origin and destiny of the universe and the people who inhabit that universe.

This model is useful in describing the worldview of many peoples in the world today. As Hiebert has stressed, the Church in its mission has been preoccupied with the upper and lower levels and has omitted reference to the middle layer. This traditional missionary approach has resulted from the two-tiered view of reality prevalent within Western society. Even the Christian missionary has preferred to ignore notions of spirits, ghosts, and astral forces, rather than recognise the importance that these matters have in the lives of the vast majority of people in the world.

An integrated theology of mission must address itself to all aspects of life. People need to realise that the kingdom of God is not merely some theological ideal relevant to the upper layer, but a practical reality which can touch every part of a person's life. Many people are bound by darkness, sickness and spiritual powers, and they must come to know Christ as Lord in these areas of their lives, as in every other. This will require an encounter of powers as the kingdom of God displaces the powers of this present age: 'because our gospel came to you not simply with words, but also with power, with the Holy Spirit and with deep conviction' (I Thess 1:5).

A word of caution here: The recognition of the supernatural in the missionary task must not lead to a preoccupation with it. The kingdom of God comes in to meet the needs of the whole person, and an obsession with one or other aspect of the nature of man can frequently lead to error. As C S Lewis wisely writes, 'There are two equal and opposite errors into which our race can fall about devils. One is to disbelieve in their existence. The other is to believe, and to feel an excessive and unhealthy interest in them. They

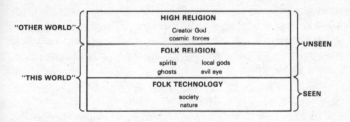

Fig 22:2

Modification of Hiebert's Analysis of the
Three-Tiered View of Reality

themselves are equally pleased by both errors, and hail a materialist or a magician with the same delight.'[7]

Discussion Questions

1 What are the fundamentals of your own worldview and how do they affect your openness to the supernatural?

2 How do you react to the statement: 'Western Christian missions have been one of the greatest secularising forces in history'? On what bases would you either agree or disagree with this comment?

3 Carefully read Luke 10:17-20 and discuss its implications.

4 Discuss the importance of spiritual discernment. What is the source of such discernment?

Recommended Reading

Michael Green, *I Believe in Satan's Downfall* (Hodder & Stoughton: London, 1981).

Merrill F Unger, *Demons in the World Today* (Tyndale House Publishers: Illinois, 1971).

David Watson, *Hidden Warfare* (STL Books: London, 1972).

Paul G Hiebert, 'Folk Religion in Andhra Pradesh', Vinay Samuel & Chris Sugden, *Evangelism and the Poor*, editors, (Paternoster: Exeter, 1983), pp 87-96.

Footnotes

1   P M John 'Reaching the Gonjas', *Worldwide* (March/April 1986) p 4.

2   Charles H Kraft, *Christianity in Culture* (Orbis Books: New York, 1979) p 121.

3   William Irvin Thompson, *Evil & World Order* (Simon & Schuster: New York, 1976) p 81.

4   Martin Lloyd-Jones, *The Christian Warfare* (Banner of Truth: London, 1976) p 6.

5   Michael Green, *I Believe in Satan's Downfall* (Hodder & Stoughton: London, 1981) pp 148-194.

6   Paul Hiebert, 'Folk Religion in Andhra Pradesh'. Vinay Samuel & Chris Sugden, *Evangelism and the Poor* (Paternoster Press: Exeter, 1983) pp 86-96.

7   See C S Lewis, *The Screwtape Letters* (Collins: London, 1965) p 9.

23

THE KINGDOM IN THE WORLD

A group of devout Christians once lived in a small village at the foot of a mountain. A winding, slippery road with hairpin curves and steep precipices without guard rails wound its way up one side of the mountain and down the other. There were frequent fatal accidents. Deeply saddened by the injured people who were pulled from the wrecked cars, the Christians in the village's three churches decided to act. They pooled their resources and purchased an ambulance so that they could rush the injured to the hospital in the next town. Week after week church volunteers gave faithfully, even sacrificially of their time to operate the ambulance twenty-four hours a day. They saved many lives although some victims remained crippled for life.

Then one day a visitor came to town. Puzzled, he asked why they did not close the road over the mountain and build a tunnel instead. Startled at first, the ambulance volunteers quickly pointed out that this approach (although technically quite possible) was not realistic or advisable. After all, the narrow mountain road had been there for a long time. Besides, the mayor would bitterly oppose the idea. (He owned a large restaurant and service station halfway up the mountain.)

The visitor was shocked that the mayor's economic interests mattered more to these Christians than the many human casualties. Somewhat hesitantly, he suggested that perhaps the churches ought to speak to the mayor. After all, he was an elder in the oldest church in town. Perhaps they should even elect a different mayor if he proved stubborn and unconcerned. Now the Christians were shocked. With rising indignation and righteous conviction they informed the young radical that the church dare not become involved in politics. The church is called to preach

*the gospel and give a cup of cold water. Its mission is not to
dabble in worldly things like social and political structures.*

*Perplexed and bitter, the visitor left. As he wandered out of
the village, one question churned round and round in his
muddled mind. Is it really more spiritual, he wondered, to
operate the ambulances which pick up the bloody victims of
destructive social structures than try to change the structures
themselves.*[1]

In a comparison of the people of Israel and the Church of
today there is one major point of contrast. Judaism was not
just a religion, but the focus of the national life of the Jewish
people and their civilisation. Judaism embraced a people in
their own land with their own culture and state. Christianity
has in the past fulfilled a similar role for the European
peoples, but today Christians are in a minority in most
countries of the world. The great question for the Christians
of today is how do they relate to the basically non-Christian
societies in which they live? What influence can the kingdom of God have upon the cultures of the world, with
respect to the political and economic aspects of a culture?
How should Christians relate to present-day pluralist societies?

Christ and Culture
H Richard Niebuhr in his book *Christ and Culture*[2] has
made what has now become a classic analysis of the various
relationships that Christianity has made with culture. He
identifies five views that have been held by Christians re-
garding their relationship to the social and political environment, and to these Niebuhr ascribes the all-embracing term
'culture'.
Christ against culture This radical position identified culture
with *kosmos* ('the world') as used in such passages as I John
2:15-16 and 5:19. In such passages Christians are warned
against loving 'the world', since it is in the power of the evil
one. It is therefore assumed that God is against the whole of

human culture. The essence of 'culture' is regarded as the evil system that the Christian sees around him, and the way to holiness is to escape from and condemn 'the world'.

Although this view rightly emphasises that Satan makes use of human culture for his own ends, it makes a number of errors. First, it assumes that culture is basically an external reality which can be left behind by a person. The anthropological understanding of the concept of culture stresses the fact that it is a learned phenomenon, and is therefore internal as well as external. Our culture is within us and so cannot be left by moving into a closed community. Even within a Christian community various social structures will emerge to form another culture. That culture may be freer from some of the sins of the former culture, but it will still be a culture, and Satan can still work through and in that way of life.

This approach equates the term 'culture' with only the negative use of the word *kosmos* in the New Testament and neglects those statements where God is said to love the *kosmos* (John 3:16). John does not use *kosmos* in I John 2:15-16 with specific reference to the whole of culture, but only to a particular use of culture by evil forces.

Christ of culture The other extreme from the 'Christ against culture' position is that of 'Christ of culture' (see figure 23:1). This view determines that God is contained either within cultures in general or within one specific culture. This view has been held by Christian gnostics such as Abelard and Ritschl.

Most commonly, advocates of this view argue that God endorses one particular culture — usually their own! This was, and still is, the view of many Jews who see God as related to their culture alone. This was the centre of the debate in Acts 15 (discussed in chapter 19). The danger here is to be blind to the failings of one's own culture while seeing the faults within others.

The alternative is to attempt to establish the perfect community. Certain Christian groups have sought to produce the ideal Christian culture, as the forerunners of the kingdom of God here on Earth. This may only be achieved

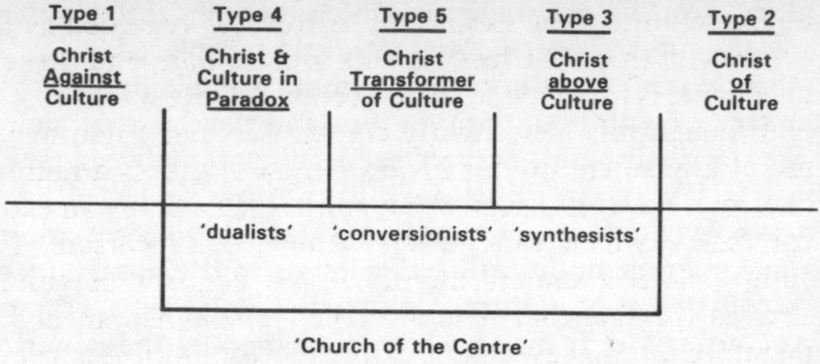

Type 1	Type 4	Type 5	Type 3	Type 2
Christ **Against** Culture	Christ & Culture in **Paradox**	Christ **Transformer** of Culture	Christ **above** Culture	Christ **of** Culture

'dualists'   'conversionists'   'synthesists'

'Church of the Centre'

Fig 23:1

Views of Christ and Culture

by forming communities in isolation from others. This view correctly understands the need for Christians to be separated from sinful structures. It recognises the fact that Jesus said of his disciples that they were not 'of the world', but it fails to see the importance of Christians being 'in the world'. How can salt affect the food unless it is dispersed within it?

Christ above culture Niebuhr also calls this view 'synthesis', and ascribes the position to Justin Martyr, Clement of Alexandria, and Thomas Aquinas. Here Christ is seen as the fulfilment of cultural aspirations and the restorer of the institutions of true society. The Christian is therefore accountable to follow the requirements of both Christ and culture, but both in their own place.

Advocates of this position point to Scripture passages such as Matthew 22:21: 'Give to Caesar what is Caesar's, and to God what is God's.' History is regarded as a synthesis of the two elements which are regarded as 'both-and' rather than 'either-or'.

Christ and culture in paradox This position has many similarities with the previous view in recognising that man must relate to both Christ and culture. However, here the two factors are seen as dualistic, and between which the individual finds himself continually in a place of tension. The Christian is a person living in two realms. Everything in the

223

present world is a paradox to which the only real solutions lie in the future when the present world is replaced.

Christ the transformer of culture Niebuhr's final approach has similarities with both the synthesis and the dualistic views. Like the dualists, it holds a clear distinction between God's work in Christ and man's work in culture. Sin has affected the whole of culture, but unlike the dualists who see culture as beyond redemption, this view holds to the possibility of the conversion of culture. Culture is seen to be corrupted but convertible. It may even be redeemed by the power of God and used for his purposes.

Augustine, Calvin, and Wesley have expounded such views. Recent writers such as Charles Kraft[3] have sought to develop this view in the light of modern anthropological insights. The strength of this transformation model is that it gives a proper understanding of the work of Christ in the incarnation as well as in that of creation. The Word became flesh and dwelt among us, and in so doing entered into human culture. This particular model of Christ the transformer of culture may be recognised as latent throughout this book.

The Church and State

These various approaches to an understanding of the relationship of culture to the Church have lead to two apparently extreme and contradictory positions with regard to the Church's involvement in political and economic systems. There have been those who have drawn strict lines between the Church and the political world. Luther with his 'two kingdoms' doctrine saw the Church and political organisations as two distinct spheres of life. The other extreme is that the Church should be involved in every aspect of human experience, and this was the basis on which the medieval popes became so involved in political issues.

Because it is a social reality with a visible institutional form, the Church is part of the political scene. The state cannot therefore totally ignore the Church. Every church finds itself in one of three particular relationships to the state: Either the state is hostile, or it is allied to the Church, or it is neutral. We must consider these three broad positions, as they affect the church and its mission.

The church frequently confronts hostility as it expands into a new area of the world. All cultures have some religion or ideology to which they are committed, and to which the political rulers relate. When a new religion enters that society it becomes a threat to the status quo, and the stability of both the political and religious leaders. Once the Early Church began to make an impact upon the Roman Empire it was regarded as a threat to the religious institutions which already existed, and the state persecuted the Church. Likewise, with Islamic societies the adherence is strongly to Islam, and with Communist countries the adherence is to atheistic Marxism. These societies therefore seek to repress the Church.

In such situations the convert is faced with various possibilities, none of which is pleasant: to flee; to compromise and become a secret believer; or to practise openly his new faith and risk punishment.

In countries which oppress Christianity, the believer is continually faced with the tension of what he should 'render to Caesar', and what to God. How far should he go in submitting to the authorities as taught in Romans 13:1-7, and how far should he resist and disobey (Acts 5:29)? Every believer must recognise those issues which are essential to his faith, and beyond compromise, and must then hold firm in the face of persecution. A demonstration of Christian love even towards one's persecutors may be the most important witness that the Christian can demonstrate in such a situation.

But what about countries in which the state is allied to the Church? From the period of Constantine, the Church in Europe has mainly been in a constitutional relationship with the state. As the various tribes of Europe became Christian, they did so with a unity of commitment known as a 'people movement'.[4] This commitment both to their tribe, and their new religion leads naturally to the alliance of Church and state. Although the Church and state had different functions in Europe, together they helped form the cultural values of Christendom.

In the Islamic societies of the world, the state and Islam are even more closely allied than has ever been true in Christianity.[5] This is because Islam is very much a religion of law (*shariah*), and herein lies one of the major points of confusion between Muslims and Christians. The Muslim looks at Western society which still calls itself Christian and considers all that he sees as a demonstration of Christianity. This is how he regards his own Islamic society − soundly based upon the religion of Islam. He therefore applies the same analysis to the West, and in condemning the immorality that he sees in the West, he also rejects the Christian religion.

In Europe, the Church frequently became manifest as the established state Church. For example, the Church of England still remains the established Church in England, and as such has some relationship to the laws of the state even though this has led to tensions in recent years. The non-Conformist churches, on the other hand, have had considerable freedom to operate within their own realm. Both the state Church and the non-Conformist churches have the responsibility for moral teaching and evangelism in order to produce a religious and law-abiding community, while the state is responsible for providing a stable, just, and healthy society.

The Scriptures do not condemn any such relationship, but there are some repercussions of which the Church is often unaware. First, the Church becomes allied in the minds of the people with the status quo. If the government in some way becomes corrupt, or seems to be unjust by some section of society, the Church is condemned with the state, as happened in the breakdown of the Holy Roman Empire. Secondly, the Church may become part of the establishment not only in its relationship, but also in the way it thinks of itself. The Church becomes the centre of tradition, and so becomes an institution rather than a dynamic community of the kingdom of God.

In some countries the state takes a neutral position with regard to religion. This view of the secular state came into being in Europe in the seventeenth and eighteenth centuries, as a result of the reaction from the years of religious wars that had occurred on the Continent. The emphasis is placed upon the right of the individual to practise his own religion provided that it does not entail anything which is contrary to the law of the land. The American constitution embodies this position as a major aspect of its Constitution. It has also been adopted in the UN Declaration of Human Rights which states: '(1) everyone shall have the right to freedom of thought, conscience, and religion; (2) freedom to manifest one's religion or belief'.[6]

The outcome is that the tolerance and neutrality of the state leads to an encouragement of a pluralism of religion within society. Christians, Muslims, Buddhists, agnostics, and outright atheists have an equal standing before the state. This view places religion into the orb of the private and personal life and leaves social and political issues with the state. In such Christian countries, the Church becomes the place for moral teaching, not for political comment.

The Christian in Society

Across the world, the Church can be seen to face each of these three positions. There is no fully developed theology of social order in the Scriptures. However, what can be seen is the influence of the Church penetrating into society as salt and light, to bring wholeness and health to society. As others have stated,[7] Christians are called to do three things with regard to the state:

Pray for the rulers of their countries '. . . I urge, then, first of all, that petitions, prayers, intercession and thanksgivings be made for everyone — for kings and all those in authority . . .' (I Tim 2:1, 2).

Submit to governments 'Everyone must submit himself to the governing authorities, for there is no authority except that which God has established. The authorities that exist have been established by God' (Rom 13:1, and also verses 2-7). This passage has been the centre of much debate which goes beyond the scope of this book. However, certain comments must be made. First, it should never be a matter of peace at

227

any price. God is a God of justice. Secondly, violence invites the response of violence.

Challenge to expose evil Social corruption must be exposed, as seen in the ministry of the prophets. Only in this way may the community of the King be salt and light in the transforming of society.

One example of this need for the challenging of present-day social corruption is with regard to the issue of wealth and poverty, introduced in chapter 1. The Church cannot and must not be silent in the face of injustice and oppression. The crippling poverty found in so many nations of the South must not be ignored by the Christians of the rich dominant nations of the North. Nor is it sufficient for Western Christians to be concerned merely with giving aid to the poor of the world. They must seek to discover the root causes of the poverty and attempt to correct them. This may require advocating changes in political and economic structures. Willy Brandt, in his preface to *North-South: a Programme for Survival*[8] sees 'North-South relations as the great social challenge of our time. We want to emphasise our belief that the two decades ahead of us may be fateful for mankind. We want responsible world citizens everywhere to realise that many global issues will come to a head in this period.'

If the Christian believes that Christ is the transformer of culture, he also must be a part of that process of transformation. He must be seeking the redeeming of the social structures of his own society and not merely the redemption of his fellow human beings. In this manner, the Christian is not only involved with the fulfilling of the redemption mandate, but also of the wider cultural mandate.

Discussion Questions
1 What should the Christian position be concerning lying when questioned by hostile government authorities? Would you accept any difference in standard when looking at the three relationships of state and church listed above?

2 What can Christians from the so-called 'free world' do for their suffering brethren in other countries?

3 What do you consider should be the Christian attitude to unjust economic structures? If you were a foreign missionary how and what would you teach the local church? Remember that you are a guest in that country.

4 What are the major social issues in your area? What are the real needs of the people concerned and how may you be part of the answer?

Recommended Reading

Richard H Niebuhr, *Christ and Culture* (Harper & Row: New York, 1951).

John Gladwin, *God's People in God's World* (IVP: Leicester, 1979).

Waldron Scott, *Bring Forth Justice* (Marshall, Morgan & Scott: London, 1980).

Vinay Samuel & Chris Sugden, Eds, *Evangelism and the Poor* (Paternoster: Exeter, 1982).

Michael Paget-Wilkes, *Poverty, Revolution and the Church* (Paternoster: Exeter, 1981).

Jim Wallis, *The Call to Conversion* (Lion Publishing: Tring, 1981).

Footnotes

1 From Morgan Derham and Ian Prior, editors, *Tear Fund Activity Book*.

2 Richard Niebuhr, *Christ & Culture* (Harper & Row Publications: New York, 1951).

3 Charles H Kraft, *Christianity in Culture* (Orbis Books: New York, 1979).

4 Donald McGavran *Bridges of God* (World Dominion Press: London, 1955).

5 N J A Coulson *A History of Islamic Law* (Edinburgh University Press: Edinburgh, 1964).

6 *UN Declaration of Human Rights*, Article 13, Paris, 1948.

7   John Gladwin, *God's People in God's World* (IVP: Leicester, 1979) pp 156-161.

8   W Brandt, *North-South: Programme for Survival* (Pan Books Ltd: London, 1980).

24

OMEGA POINT

The Damal people live in a remote area of Iryan Jaya, and have only recently been reached with the Gospel. Even so, they already have an awareness of their missionary responsibility, as this song reveals.

> *'Come, Holy Spirit, and fill us with Your power.*
> *Come, oh counselor, and give us help.*
> *Send us forth with the message of Jesus' resurrection.*
> *That we Damals may tell the message boldly.*
> *Send us to people who have not tasted the sweet potato of life.*
> *Many sweet potatoes are mature and ready to be harvested*
> *Come, my comrades, let us dig the potato harvest.*
> *When the last sweet potato has been dug*
> *We will enter the beautiful gate with joy and singing.*
> *Come, Holy Spirit, and fill us with your power.'*[1]

The missionary responsibilities of the people of God were described in the first chapter as like a stream rising in the mountains and gradually flowing to the sea. On the journey one sees the river of obligation growing in width and depth (see figure 1:3). However, there is always the danger that one can be so preoccupied with the actual practice of these responsibilities, that one forgets the task is to accomplish an ultimate purpose. A time will come when the mission will have been fulfilled.

In recent years it has not been fashionable for the Church to speak about the 'last things'. The little man carrying a placard bearing the words 'The End is Near' has become a figure of fun. Even many leading theologians have rejected the notion. Bultmann has written, 'It is no longer possible for anyone seriously to hold the New Testament view of the World . . . we can no longer look for the return of the Son of Man on the clouds of heaven or hope that the faithful will meet him in the air.'[2]

Both Protestant and Roman Catholic theologians have stressed concern for immediate problems relating to current issues in this world. The taunt that religion is merely 'pie in the sky when you die' has seemed to keep many Christians from seeing the significance of the Second Coming as the climax of world history. It has been left to the secular scholars to focus attention on the future. Since 1970, the fastest growing subject in the American universities has been futurology. Statistics and computer studies have been used to extrapolate current data, and so give some picture of the possible future of the world.[3] Many of these studies have shown a fearful picture of what could happen to our world, and it is therefore not without reason that many young people are deeply concerned.

Dr J Bronowski ended his book *The Ascent of Man* with the words, 'I am infinitely saddened to find myself suddenly surrounded by a terrible loss of nerve.'[4] How did this pessimism arise? The nineteenth century was largely characterised by a confident view of man's abilities resulting from growing economic and technological development among the Western nations. However, two devastating wars left these same nations perplexed about their own abilities, and with the realisation that the technological revolution was the opening of a Pandora's box. With the advent of atomic power people suddenly realised that nuclear fission had given humankind the power to destroy utterly life on Earth. The haunting trepidation of possible nuclear destruction led to an increasing pessimism that was further stimulated by the population explosion and news of extensive famines. The depleting resources of the Earth, especially that of oil, have compounded the fears of many. The bright golden future of yesterday has for many become a doom watch — the omega point!

In the midst of this loss of confidence many have come to feel that the Church needs to rediscover its sense of history. The world will not come to a pathetic end with someone pushing a button that starts a nuclear holocaust. God has a plan that is being worked out. He is in control. It is God's mission, and the Church needs to once again recapture the excitement of her destiny and mission.

Signs of the End

Intensification of Evil

In a study of eschatology a number of important themes all converge together. The first is that in the end times there will be an intensification of evil. There are many indications of this in the New Testament. Wars, famines, plagues, declining morals, totalitarian rule, and false prophets are all mentioned in some detail.

These forebodings have led to a sense of despair among Christians as well as others in the Western world and have had the subtle effect of lowering our expectations for the growth of the Church. At a time when the nations are in greatest need, the Church has lost confidence in her mission and sees herself as a tiny remnant. The New Testament prophecies about the intensification of evil are not made to spread gloom and despondency but to foster realism about the malignancy of evil and to encourage faith, patience and hope. The book of Revelation is a graphic account of how all the horses and their riders, the beast and the anti-Christ cannot prevent God fulfilling his purpose — the eventual climax of the crowd which no man could number gathering around the throne of God. The paradox expounded here is that the mission of the Church will be culminated in the context of an evil world. Irrespective of the world situation, the Church is destined to fulfil her mission, whether it be from a concentration camp or an air-conditioned house. Our methods may change, but our mission and the sense of urgency to accomplish that task must remain.

To All People

A second major theme in the study of eschatology is the necessity for the Gospel to be proclaimed to all people. In giving the Great Commission our Lord saw the task of making disciples from all people as stretching from that time until the very end of the age. He saw the mission growing out from that group of disciples into Judea and Samaria, and then the furthest part of the Earth (Acts 1:8): 'And the gospel must first be preached to all nations.' (Mark 13:10). God's plan is that before the end there will be a worldwide preaching of the Gospel. This was a major motivation in the missionary expansion of the last century. Evangelical missionaries would speak of 'bringing back the King'.

We must also question what is meant by Mark 13:10 and also Matthew 24:14, 'And this gospel of the Kingdom will be preached in the whole world, as a testimony to all nations, and then the end will come.' This is the goal towards which the people of God should be moving in their mission, and which should guide their mission strategy. But, what is meant by the phrase 'all people' to whom we are to preach the Gospel and from whom we are to make disciples; and, when do we consider that the Gospel has been adequately preached?

In dealing with the first question it is necessary to note that in Mark 13:10 the words used are *ta ethna,* meaning distinct sociological groups. This is basically the same concept as was recognised in the Old Testament. Although God chose Israel as his people he did not forget the promise that was given to Abraham (Gen 12:3) that blessing would come to all the nations. This concept is further expanded in the book of Revelation where several series of expressions are used to describe those who are gathered around the throne of God. Revelation 7:9: 'After this I looked, and there before me was a great multitude that no one could count, from every nation, tribe, people and language, standing before the throne and in front of the Lamb. They were wearing white robes and were holding palm branches in their hands.' In each of the seven descriptive listings in Revelation several terms are used to provide a repetition and balance to the verse (See Rev 5:9, 7:9, 10:11, 11:9, 13:7, 14:6, 17:15). The terms are used to denote a variety of concepts, 'people' – a cultural term; 'nation', 'tribe' – racial terms; 'language' – linguistic; 'multitude' – demographic; and 'Kings' – a personification of kingdoms, and political countries. Humankind is seen as a complex mosaic, and into each of these groups the Gospel will have been proclaimed.

The second question relates to when we may consider a people to have been evangelised. The Revelation passages reveal that more than a verbal communication of the message will have occurred. It will have resulted in there being Christians from every people group gathered around the throne of God. Perhaps it is easier for this reason to define what is meant by an unevangelised, or unreached people. The Lausanne Continuation Committee has proposed the following definition of an unreached people: 'a people group among which there is no indigenous community of believing Christians with adequate numbers and resources to evangelise this people without outside (cross-cultural) assistance.'[5] Although this description leaves some aspects aside, it does provide a practical definition and highlights the remaining missionary task of the Church.

Judgement

A third major theme of the Scriptures concerning the end of the age is that there will be a judgement. The extended simile given by our Lord in Matthew 25:31-46 compares the judgement of the nations with the separating of a mixed flock of sheep and goats. The story presents an unequivocable picture of a separation of mankind into two groups with two destinies. Although one may like to be comforted by the possibility of the ultimate universal salvation of all, an honest reading of the Scriptures does not allow this. The future judgement of all people by their Creator is a fact of Scripture which cannot be denied without doing a radical injustice to the biblical text.

The doctrine of hell has been criticised by many during this century. It has been regarded as old-fashioned and outside the New Testament revelation of God as a God of love. They would argue that Jesus came to demonstrate the love of God. Yet it is this same Jesus who speaks most about hell in the whole of Scripture. The words used by Jesus may

235

seem figurative, but the picture that is left in one's mind is quite clear: 'They will throw them into the fiery furnace, where there will be weeping and gnashing of teeth' (Matt 13:42; 13:50; 22:13; 24:51; 25:30). The picture is that of a banquet which is held at night. The wicked are thrust out from the light, joy and festivity into the darkness and gloom.

The basic principle of judgement is the inherent justice of God: 'Will not the Judge of all the earth do right?' (Gen 18:25) Jesus taught that the destiny of people rested upon their attitude to him, '. . . you do not believe the one he sent. You diligently study the Scriptures because you think that by them you possess eternal life. These are the Scriptures that testify about me, yet you refuse to come to me and to have life' (John 5:38).

It is, however, necessary to add that those who have been justified by faith in Christ will in fact also stand before the judgement seat of Christ (II Cor 5:10). Because of their redemption in Christ that Day will loose its terror (I John 4:17). The judgement of believers will reveal the quality of their work, and this applies to the Christian seeking to fulfil the mission of God: '. . . the Day will bring it to light. It will be revealed with fire, and the fire will test the quality of each man's work' (I Cor 3:10-15).

New Heaven and a New Earth

To focus on judgement can naturally lead to the conclusion that the world is beyond redemption and that the only solution is for the total destruction of the world and a new start. There are many verses of Scripture that indicate cataclysmic happenings in earth and heaven associated with the coming of the Lord. Peter uses graphic pictures of an earth that is burnt up and everything destroyed with it: 'By the same word the present heavens and the earth are preserved for fire, being kept for the day of judgement and destruction of ungodly men' (II Pet 3:7).

However, there are also verses in Scripture which point not to a total destruction and new creation, but to a continuity. The New Testament Greek word *palingenesia (palin,* again; *genesis*, birth) is translated by the English expression 'new birth'. This is the very word used by Jesus in Matthew 19:28: '. . . at the renewal of all things, when the Son of Man sits on his glorious throne . . .' He is using it here in the wider sense, of the regeneration of all things. The word *apokatasis* (*apo*, back; *kathistemi*, to set in order) is translated to restore, and is used in Acts 3:21: 'He must remain in heaven until the time comes for God to restore everything, as he promised long ago through his holy prophets.'

A passage that says much about this process of recreation is I Corinthians 15:35-56. Paul here uses the illustration of a seed that is sown and the plant that springs from the seed. Just as the plant is different from the seed, and yet came out of the very essence of the seed, so the resurrected body will be related to that of our present human body. Likewise, creation is to be liberated and transformed, not destroyed. There is an element of mystery over this whole aspect of recreation in just the same way as there is a sense of wonder at a dry seed growing into a living plant. A world marked by evil and misuse by man will somehow be transformed and will 'be liberated from its bondage to decay and brought into the glorious freedom of the children of God' (Rom 8:21).

This element of continuity highlights an additional dimension to our life here on earth. This world becomes a training ground as to how we will live and what responsibilities we will have in the 'new earth'. The well known parable of the talents seeks to express this very point. The faithfulness of the servants fits them for the tasks under new conditions (Matt 25:14-30; Luke 19:11-27). The mission of the people of God therefore takes on an eschatological value, and not just one of immediate value. As Billheimer has written, 'the entire universe under the Son's regulation and control is being [directed] by God for one purpose — to prepare and train the Bride.'[6]

The New Jerusalem

The image of the New Jerusalem coming down out of heaven from God, the climatic event of history, is set forth in Revelation 21:1-22:5. It brings together all the prophetic strands of Scripture and unites God, his people, heaven and earth into a single glorious unity.

The centre of John's vision is the fact that God's dwelling is now with man. This is not a passage for speculation or theories. It is an apocalyptic vision in which the writer is struggling with human language to describe the indescribable. This is a passage which should provoke wonder rather than analysis as it draws all the great symbolic pictures of the Scriptures into one glorious vision of cosmic reconciliation.

The New Jerusalem stretches human imagination. It is described as a perfect cube 2,400 kilometres along each side. It is made of the most precious of materials. The consummation of both Old and New Testament elements is seen in the symbolism of the names of the twelve tribes of Israel written over the gates of the city, and the names of the apostles providing the foundation stones. In the city there is no temple and no sun because the glory of God is in the midst. God will reveal himself completely in a perfect relationship with his creation.

Now the people of God who have suffered, been persecuted, and known pain will be satisfied: 'He will wipe every tear from their eyes. There will be no more death or mourning or crying or pain, for the old order of things has passed away' (Rev 21:4).

Into this city will be brought the 'glory and honour of the nations' (Rev 21:24, 26). Here the richness of human culture and creativity is gathered into the New World. The best of human culture will not be lost, but will be purified and purged of all sin (Rev 21:27). 'Now the dwelling of God is with men, and he will live with them. They will be his people, God himself will be with them and be their God' (Rev 21:3). God will have gathered unto himself a people! This is one of the great missionary themes that unite the whole panorama of the mission of God.

The throne of God and of the Lamb will be in the city, and his servants will serve him. They will see his face, and his name will be on their foreheads.

There will be no more night. They will not need the light of a lamp or the light of the sun, for the Lord God will give them light. And they will reign for ever and ever.

(Rev 22:3-5)

Discussion Questions
1 How does the future prospect of the judgement affect your views and attitude to mission?
2 Seek to identify some people groups that may be described as 'unreached'. You may want to refer to *Operation World* (STL & WEC International: London, 1986).
3 What riches of your culture would you consider acceptable to God?

Recommended Reading
Tom Sine, *The Mustard Seed Conspiracy* (MARC Europe: London, 1985).
John Stott, Ed, *The Year 2000 AD* (Marshall, Morgan & Scott: London, 1983).
Alvin Toffler, *Future Shock* (Pan Books: London, 1971).
Donella H Meadow, Ed, *The Limits to Growth* (Pan Books: London, 1972).
Francis A Schaeffer, *The Church at the End of the Twentieth Century* (Norfolk Press: London, 1970).

Footnotes
1 Alice Gibbons, *The People Time Forgot* (Moody Press: Chicago, 1981), p 323.
2 Rudolf Bultman, *Jesus Christ and Mythology* (SCM Press: London, 1960) p 38.
3 Donella H Meadows, *Limits to Growth* (Pan Books: London, 1972).
4 Jacob Bronowski, *The Ascent of Man* BBC Publications: London, 1973.
5 Edward R Dayton and Samuel Wilson, *The Future of*

World Evangelization (Unreached Peoples '84) MARC Europe: London, 1985) p129.

6   Paul K Billheimer, *Destined for the Throne* (CLC: London, 1975) p 27.

SELECTED
BIBLIOGRAPHY

ALLAN, E L. *Christianity among the Religions*. SCM Press: London, 1960.

ALLEN, Roland. *St. Paul's Methods & Ours*. World Dominion: London, 1953.

ANDERSON, Sir Norman. *Christianity and World Religions*. IVP: Leicester, 1984.

BARRETT, David. *World Christian Encylopaedia*. Oxford University Press: Oxford, 1982.

BAVINCK, J N. *An Introduction to the Science of Mission*. Presbyterian & Reformed Pub Co: Philadelphia, 1960.

BERGER, P L. *Pyramids of Sacrifice*. Pelican Books: London, 1977.

BERKHOF, Louis. *Systematic Theology*. Banner of Truth Trust: London, 1959.

BILLHEIMER, Paul K. *Destined for the Throne*. CLC: London, 1975.

BLAUW, J. *The Missionary Nature of the Church*. Lutterworth Press: London, 1962.

BLOCHES, Jacques. 'Mission — And Proselytism', in LINDSELL, Harold, editor, *The Church's Worldwide Mission*. Word Books: Waco, 1966: p 112.

BLOCH, Ernest. *Man on His Own*. Herder & Herder: New York, 1970.

BONHOEFFER, Deitrich. *Ethics*. MacMillan: New York, 1965.

BRIDGES, Donald & PHYPERS, David. *Spiritual Gifts & the Church*. IVP: Leicester, 1973.

Brong Ahafo Regional Congress on Evangelism. New Life For All: Accra, 1985.

BRIGHT, John. *The History of Israel*. SCM Press: London, 1974.

BRIEGGEMANN, W. *Tradition for Crises*. John Knox Press: Edinburgh, 1968.

BRONOWSKI, Jacob. *The Ascent of Man*. BBC Publications: London, 1973.

BROWN, Robert. *Religion — Origin & Ideas*. Tyndale Press: London, 1966.

BUDGE, Wallis E A. *Egyptian Religion*. Routledge & Kegan Paul: London, 1899.

BULTMAN, Rudolf. *Jesus Christ & Mythology*. SCM Press: London, 1960.

CALVIN, John. *Commentaries on the Book of Genesis* Vol 1, Calvin Translation Society: Edinburgh, 1847: p 91.

CAREY, William. 'An Enquiry into the Obligation of Christians . . .' in WINTER, Ralph, editor, *Perspectives on the World Christian Movement — a Reader*. William Carey Library: Pasadena, 1981: pp 227-237.

COTTERELL, Peter. *The Eleventh Commandment*. IVP: Leicester, 1981.

COULSON, N J A. *A History of Islamic Law*. Edinburgh University Press: Edinburgh, 1964.

CULLMANN, Oscar. *Christ & Time*. SCM Press: London, 1951.

DAYTON, Edward R & WILSON, Samuel. *The Future of World Evangelisation (Unreached Peoples '84)*. MARC: Pasadena, 1984.

DeRIDDER, Richard H. *Discipling the Nations*. Baker Book House: Grand Rapids, 1975.

DeLANGE, Nicholas. *Atlas of the Jewish World*. Phaidon Press: Oxford, 1984.

DOWLEY & MARSH. *Explaining the Gospel in Today's World*. Scripture Union: London 1982. pp 14-48.

ENTZ, Loren. 'Challenge to Abou's Jesus.' *Evangelical Missions Quarterly* Vol 22 No 1 (1986) pp 46-50.

ESCOBAR, Samuel. 'Evangelism & Man's Search for Freedom, Justice & Fulfilment.' *Let the Earth Hear His Voice*. World Wide Publications: Minneapolis, 1975; pp 303-326.

EVANS, William. *The Great Doctrines of the Bible*. Moody Press: Chicago, 1968.

Famine: A Man-made Disaster? A Report for the Independent Commission on International Humanitarian Issues. Pan Books: London, 1985.

FARQUHAR, J N. *The Crown of Hinduism.* Oxford University Press: Madras, 1915.

GLADWIN, John. *God's People in God's World.* IVP: Leicester, 1979.

GREEN, Michael. *I Believe in Satan's Downfall.* Hodder & Stoughton: London, 1981.

GRIFFITHS, Michael. 'Today's Missionaries, Yesterday's Apostles.' *Evangelical Missions Quarterly* Vol 21, No 2 (1983).

HANKS, Geoffrey. *Island of No Return – the Story of Father Daimen of Molokai.* The Religious Education Press: Oxford, 1978.

HARRISON, R K. *Introduction to the Old Testament.* Tyndale Press: London, 1970.

HIEBERT, Paul. 'Folk Religion in Andra Pradesh.' SAMUEL, Vinay & SUGDEN, Chris. *Evangelism and the Poor.* Paternoster Press: Exeter, 1983.

HODGES, Melvin. *Build My Church.* Assemblies of God Publications: Springfield, Missouri, 1957.

HODGES, Melvin. *On the Mission Field.* Moody Press: Chicago, 1957.

HONG, Silas. *The Dragon Net.* Victory Press: Eastbourne, 1976.

HOOYKAS, R. *Religion and the Rise of Modern Science.* Eerdmans: Grand Rapids, 1972.

International Review of Mission. 'Racism'. Vol 59, No 235 (1970).

JOSEPHUS, Flavius. *Antiquities.* Pickering & Inglis: London, 1960.

KEIL, C F, & DELITZSHE, F. *Commentary on the Old Testament, Vol VII, part 2.* Eerdmans: Grand Rapids, 1970.

KIRK, Andrew. 'The Kingdom of God and the Church in Contemporary Protestantism and Catholicism.' *Let the Earth Hear His Voice.* World Wide Publications: Minneapolis, 1975; pp 1071-82.

KRAEMER, Hendrick. *The Christian Message in a Non-*

Christian World. The Edinburgh House Press: London, 1938.

KRAFT, Charles. *Christianity in Culture*. Orbis Books: New York, 1979.

KUNG, Hans. *On Being a Christian*. Doubleday: New York, 1976.

KUYPER, A. *Encyclopedia of Sacred Theology*. MacMillan: New York, 1898.

KUYPER, A. *God-Centred Evangelism*. The Banner of Truth: London, 1961.

LANE, Tony. *The Lion Concise Book of Christian Thought*. Lion Publishing: Tring, 1984.

Lausanne Covenant, The. DOUGLAS J D. *Let the Earth Hear His Voice*. World Wide Publications: Minneapolis, 1974.

Lausanne Occasional Paper No 23 — Christian Witness to Nominal Christians among Protestants. LCWE: Illinois, 1980.

LEWIS, C S. *Miracles*. Geoffrey Bles: London, 1947.

LEWIS, C S. *The Problem of Pain*. Fontana Books: London, 1940.

Lion Handbook of the Bible, The. Lion Publishing: Tring, 1973.

LLOYD-JONES, Martin. *The Christian Warfare*. Banner of Truth: London, 1976.

LUTHER, Martin. *Commentary on Genesis*. (1522).

McGAVRAN, Donald. *Bridges of God*. World Dominion Press: London, 1955.

McGAVRAN, Donald. *Understanding Church Growth*. Eerdmans: Grand Rapids, 1970.

MEADOWS, Donella H. *Limits to Growth*. Pan Books: London, 1972.

MILLER, Penny. *Myths & Legends of South Africa*. Bulpin Publications: Cape Town, 1979.

NICHOLSON, Max. *Nature Conservancy*.

NIEBUHR, Richard. *Christ and Culture*. Harper & Row Publications: New York, 1951.

O'BRIAN, Peter T. 'The Great Commission of Mt 28:18-20.' *Ev Rev Theol* Vol 2, No 2 (1978).

ORR, J Edwin. 'The Outpouring of the Spirit in Revival & Awakening and Its Issues in Church Growth' Personal publication of Edwin Orr, 1984.

Partnership. No 5 (1976).

PERKINS, Harvey 'Let My People Go.' *Mission Trends No 3: Third World Theologies*. Eerdmans: Grand Rapids, 1976.

RAHNER, Karl. *Theological Investigations*, Vol 5. Darton, Longman & Todd: London, 1954.

ROWLEY, H H. *Israel's Mission to the World*. SCM Press: London, 1939.

RICHARDSON, Alan. *A Theological Word Book of the Bible*. SCM Press: London, 1950.

RICHARDSON, Don. *Eternity in Their Heart*. Regal Books: Ventura, 1981.

RICHARDSON, Don. *Peace Child*. Gospel Light: Glendale, 1974.

SCHAEFFER, Francis A. *He is There and He Is Not Silent*. Tyndale House: Wheaton, 1972.

SCHAEFFER, Francis A. *Escape From Reason*. IVP: Leicester, 1968.

SCHOFIELD, C I. *Holy Bible*. Oxford University Press: Oxford, 1945.

SCHWEITZER, Albert. *The Quest of the Historical Jesus*. A & C Black: London, 1910.

SENIOR, Donald and STUHLUMUELEER, Carroll. *The Biblical Foundations for Mission*. SCM Press: London, 1983.

SIDER, R J. *Rich Christians in an Age of Hunger*. Hodder and Stoughton: London, 1977.

SINE, Tom. *The Church in Response to Human Need*. MARC: Monrovia, 1983.

SNYDER, Howard A. *New Wineskins*. Marshall, Morgan & Scott: London, 1976.

STEINER, George. 'After Babel.' *The Listener*. April 1977: pp 510-514, 533-538.

STOTT, John. *Christian Mission in the Modern World*. Falcon Books: London, 1975.

STOTT, John. *Walk in His Shoes*. IVP: Leicester, 1975.

SWAMIDOSS, A W. 'The Biblical Basis of the Para-Church Movements.' *Evangelical Review of Theology* Vol 7, No 2 (1983).

TASKER, R G V. *New Bible Dictionary*. IVP: Leicester, 1968.

TILLICH, Paul. *Christianity and the Encounter of World Religions*. New York, 1963.

TIPPETT, Alan. *Verdict Theology in Missionary Theory*. William Carey Library: Pasadena, 1973.

THOMPSON, William Irvin. *Evil & World Order*. Simon & Schuster: New York, 1976.

TURNER, Howard W. *Profile through Preaching*. Edinburgh House Press: Edinburgh, 1965.

TYLOR, E B. *Primitive Culture*. John Murray: London, 1871.

U N Declaration of Human Rights. Paris, 1948.

WAGNER, Peter. *Frontiers in Missionary Strategy*. Moody Press: Chicago, 1971.

WAGNER, Peter. *Your Spiritual Gifts Can Help Your Church Grow*. MARC Europe: London, 1985.

WALLS, Andrews. 'Stewardship.' *Handbook on World Development*. Shaftesbury Project Publication: Nottingham, 1983: pp 82-85.

WATSON, David. *I Believe in Evangelism*. Hodder & Stoughton: London, 1976.

'Wheaton '83 Statement, Social Transformation: The Church in Response to Human Need.' *Transformation* Vol 1, No 1 (1984): pp 23-28.

WHITTAKER, Colin. *Great Revivals*. Marshalls: London, 1984.

WIMBER, John. *Power Evangelism: Signs and Wonders Today*. Hodder & Stoughton: London, 1985.

YODER, John Howard. *Politics of Jesus*. Eerdmans: Grand Rapids, 1972.

GETTING THERE FROM HERE
Elizabeth Goldsmith

Subtitled 'Mission Possible', this book — aimed mainly at young people but valuable to anyone of any age who is considering mission — provides suggestions on how to get 'there' from 'here'. Mrs Goldsmith outlines the biblical basis for mission and gives step-by-step guidance. She answers many common objections to mission such as, "Isn't there enough suffering already in our own country? Why send our best and brightest abroad?" and "Surely mission is just another form of western colonialism?".

This unusual and helpful guide will become the basic resource tool for the next generation of missionaries. It will also inspire those who think vaguely of mission as something 'over there', to reconsider their own calling.

Wittily illustrated throughout, **Getting There from Here** contains a directory to Protestant missionary societies and to Bible training courses.

The Author: Elizabeth Goldsmith is a former missionary with Overseas Missionary Fellowship and now on the staff of All Nations Christian College. She and her husband, Martin Goldsmith, have written many books on mission and related subjects.

Published jointly with STL Books and the Evangelical Missionary Alliance.

160 pp   £1.95

FRIENDSHIP ACROSS CULTURES
Tim Stafford

Tim and Popie Stafford spent four years in Kenya as missionaries, eager to learn, to be culturally sensitive and to work alongside their African partners. However, the experience proved to be extraordinarily difficult.

Signals easily get confused, the Staffords found, when cultures mix. Should you invite a national to your home? How do you give, or receive, presents? To what extent should you adopt local dress? How, above all, do you cope with 'culture fatigue' – the sheer weariness of living constantly with the unfamiliar?

Drawing on his own and others' experiences, Tim Stafford sets out invaluable rules of thumb for anyone who aspires to make friendships across cultures. His book is relevant not only to practitioners overseas, but to anyone in the western world who wishes to get to know neighbours or work contacts from a different cultural background. **Friendship Across Cultures** is a deeply felt, imaginative, easily read book which provides a valuable introduction to the task of transmitting the Christian faith worldwide.

The Author: Tim Stafford, for four years the managing editor of *Step* magazine in Nairobi, is the author of **Do You Sometimes Feel Like a Nobody?** He writes a monthly column for *Campus Life* in the USA.

Published jointly with STL Books.

144pp   £3.95

DON'T LET THE GOATS EAT THE LOQUAT TREES
Thomas Hale

The remarkable adventures of a surgeon in Nepal.

The extraordinary story of the establishment of a hospital in the mountains of Nepal. Dr Thomas Hale, an American surgeon, gives a graphic account of his struggles with climate, superstition, ignorance, insects, rugged terrain and Nepalese transport. His wry sense of humour, his vivid medical descriptions, his compassion and his profound sense of God's calling and support make this thoroughly readable book a combination between Dr Kildare, James Herriott and Hudson Taylor! Read to learn — but also to enjoy a marvellous, enthralling story.

"I have enjoyed reading this book more than any I have come across in years."
— Paul Brand, author of **Fearfully & Wonderfully Made**

"Dr Hale is an incredible storyteller, and his book is most difficult to lay aside."
— Ted Engstrom, past President,
World Vision International

"Masterfully written. A great mix of humour, pathos and love."
— Jerry White, Executive Director, The Navigators.

The Author: Dr Thomas Hale and his wife have two children and are still working in Nepal.

Published jointly with BMMF Interserve.

256pp   £2.50

THE PRISONER
AND OTHER STORIES
Rhena Taylor

Ten sharp-edged stories reflecting the reality of the mission field.

Many 'missionary' biographies fail to tell the whole truth. They play down the disagreements between colleagues, the anger of rising nationalism, the problems of insecurity and doubt. By using fiction Rhena Taylor is able to bring immediacy to the tough world of mission, and to evoke an intensity of response denied more conventional accounts. She is also able to tackle themes which must frequently be left to one side in the interest of reducing hurt.

Thus the tales in this collection throw into vivid relief acutely-observed issues; the transfer of power from a European to an African; the frustrations caused by lack of resources; corruption in a relief camp; the bitter resentment of patronising attitudes; and much else.

No one reading this book will ever think the same way about 'missionary work'. It is an important aid to understanding and prayer.

The Author: Rhena Taylor is the author of **Rough Edges** (IVP, 1978) and since 1962 has worked for the Bible Churchmen's Missionary Society in Kenya.

Published jointly with Bible Churchmen's Missionary Society.

192pp   £2.25

WHO ARE WORLD VISION?

World Vision is a major Christian relief and development agency, founded over 35 years ago. World Vision now help the hungry, the homeless, the sick and the poor in over 80 countries worldwide.

World Vision is international, interdenominational and has no political affiliation, working wherever possible through local churches and community leaders in close co-operation with the United Nations and other international relief agencies.

Childcare sponsorship is an important part of World Vision's Christian work. Over 400,000 children are currently being cared for in over 2,000 projects.

Sponsors in Europe and around the world are helping thousands of needy children by supplying food, clothing, medical care and schooling. These children usually live with their families although some are in schools or homes. Development and training are usually offered to the communities where the sponsored children live so that whole families can become self-reliant.

World Vision is able to respond with immediate and appropriate relief in crisis situations such as famines, floods, earthquakes and wars. Hundreds of thousands have been saved in Africa through feeding and medical centres. Other projects include cyclone relief for Bangladesh, relief work in Lebanon and medical assistance for Kampuchea.

Over 500 community development projects in 50 countries are helping people to help themselves towards a healthier and more stable future. These projects include agricultural and vocational training, improvements in health care and nutrition (especially for mothers and babies), instruction in hygiene, literacy classes for children and adults, development of clean water supplies and village leadership training.

World Vision's approach to aid is integrated in the sense that we believe in helping every aspect of a person's life and needs. We also help Christian leaders throughout the world to become more effective in their ministry and assist local churches in many lands with their work.

If you would like more information about the work of World Vision, please contact one of the offices listed below.

World Vision of Britain
Dychurch House
8 Abington Street
Northampton NN1 2AJ
United Kingdom
Tel: 0604 22964

World Vision Deutschland
Postfach 1848
Adenauerallee 32
D-6370 Oberursel
West Germany
Tel: 496171 56074/5/6/7

Suomen World Vision
Kalevankatu 14 C 13
00100 Helsinki 10
Finland
Tel: 358 90 603422

Stichting World Vision
   Nederland
Postbus 818
3800 AV Amersfoort
The Netherlands
Tel: 3133 10041

World Vision International
919 West Hungtington
   Drive
Monrovia, California
91016, United States of
   America
Tel: 818 303 8811

World Vision of Australia
Box 399-C, G P O
Melbourne
3001 Victoria Australia
Tel: 613 699 8522

World Vision of Ireland
17 Percy Place
Dublin 4
Eire
Tel: 0001 606 058

World Vision of New Zealand
PO Box 1923
Auckland
New Zealand
Tel: 649 770 879

World Vision Canada
6630 Turner Valley Rd
Mississauga
Ontario
Canada L5N 2S4
Tel: 416 821 3030

World Vision International
Christliches Hilfswerk
Mariahilferstrasse 10/10
A-1070 Wien Austria
Tel: 0043-222-961 333/366

World Vision International
Christliches Hilfswerk
Badenerstrasse 87
CH-8004 Zürich Switzerland
Tel: 0041-1-241 7222